GRAPHIC LIBRARY

GRAPHIC BIOGRAPHIES

BENJAMIN
AN AMERICAN GENIUS
FRANKLIN

by Kay Melchisedech Olson
illustrated by Gordon Purcell
and Barbara Schulz

Consultant:

John C. Van Horne, Director

The Library Company of Philadelphia

Philadelphia, Pennsylvania

Capstone
press

Mankato, Minnesota

Graphic Library is published by Capstone Press,
151 Good Counsel Drive, P.O. Box 669, Mankato, Minnesota 56002.
www.capstonepress.com

Printed in the United States of America

1 2 3 4 5 6 10 09 08 07 06 05

Library of Congress Cataloging-in-Publication Data
Olson, Kay Melchisedech.
Benjamin Franklin: an American genius / by Kay Melchisedech Olson; illustrated by Gordon Purcell and Barbara Schulz.
p. cm. — (Graphic library. Graphic biographies)
Summary: "In graphic novel format, tells the life story of American statesman and inventor Benjamin Franklin"—Provided by publisher.
Includes bibliographical references and index.
ISBN 0-7368-4629-8 (hardcover)
1. Franklin, Benjamin, 1706–1790—Juvenile literature. 2. Statesmen—United States—Biography—Juvenile literature. 3. Inventors—United States—Biography—Juvenile literature. 4. Scientists—United States—Biography—Juvenile literature. 5. Printers—United States—Biography—Juvenile literature. I. Purcell, Gordon, ill. II. Schulz, Barbara, (Artist) ill. III. Title. IV. Series.
E302.6.F8O465 2006
973.3'092—dc22 2005003964

Art and Editorial Direction
Jason Knudson and Blake A. Hoena

Designers
Jason Knudson and Juliette Peters

Colorist
Benjamin Hunzeker

Editor
Christine Peterson

Editor's note: Direct quotations from primary sources are indicated by a yellow background.

Direct quotations appear on the following pages:

Page 8, from *Poor Richard's Almanac* by Benjamin Franklin (Mount Vernon, N.Y.: Peter Pauper Press, 1980).

Page 18, from Franklin's letter dated July 11, 1765; page 24, from Franklin's letter dated July 27, 1783; page 27, an epitaph written by Franklin in 1728; as published in *Writings* by Benjamin Franklin, edited by J. A. Leo Lemay (New York: Literary Classics of the United States: Distributed to the trade in the United States and Canada by Viking, 1987).

Page 12, from *Benjamin Franklin* by Carl Van Doren (New York: Bramhall House, 1987).

Page 27, from *The Works of Benjamin Franklin*, edited by Jared Sparks (Boston: Hillard, Gray and Company, 1840).

TABLE OF CONTENTS

Chapter 1

PRINTER

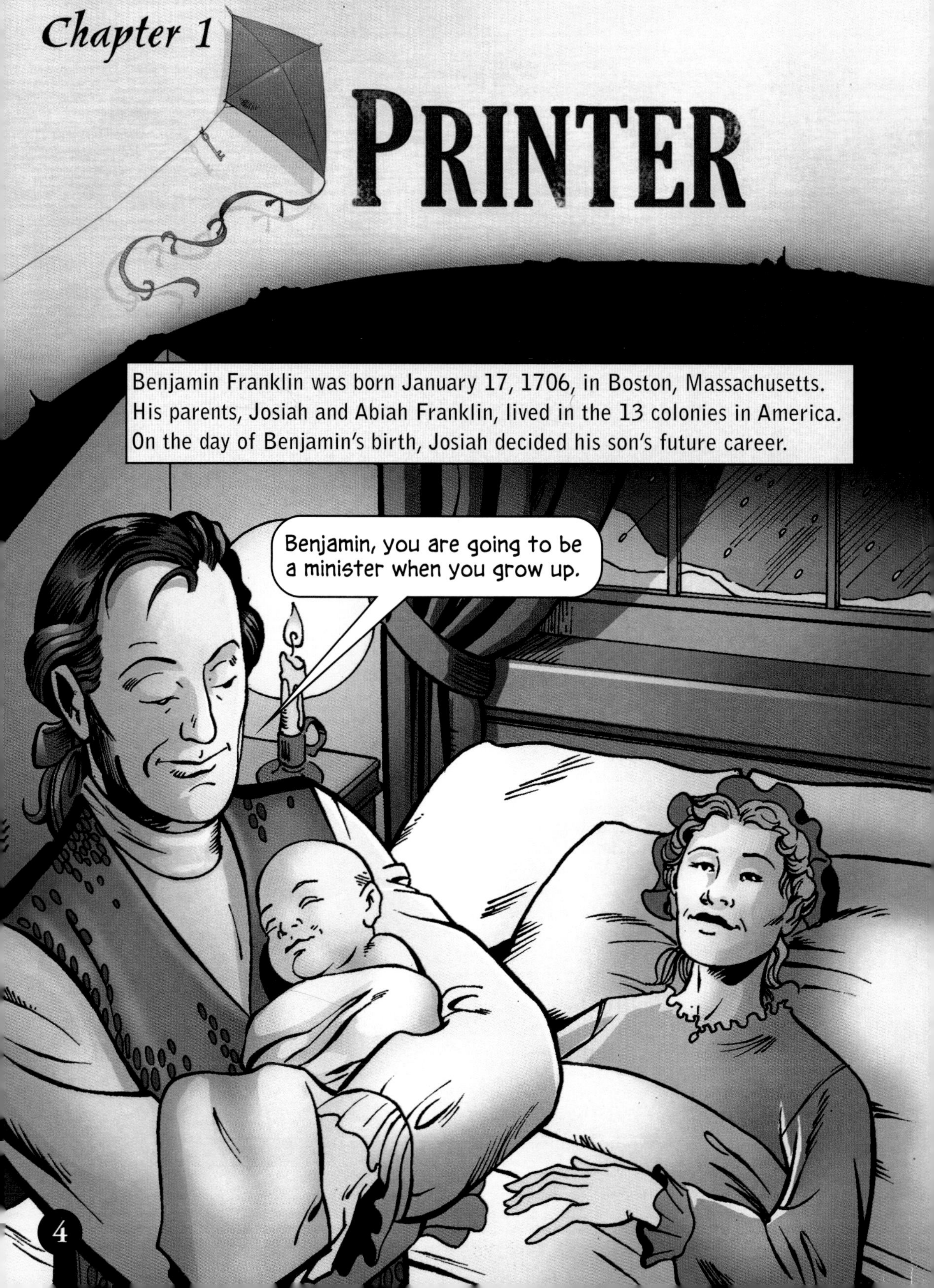
Benjamin Franklin was born January 17, 1706, in Boston, Massachusetts. His parents, Josiah and Abiah Franklin, lived in the 13 colonies in America. On the day of Benjamin's birth, Josiah decided his son's future career.
Benjamin, you are going to be a minister when you grow up.

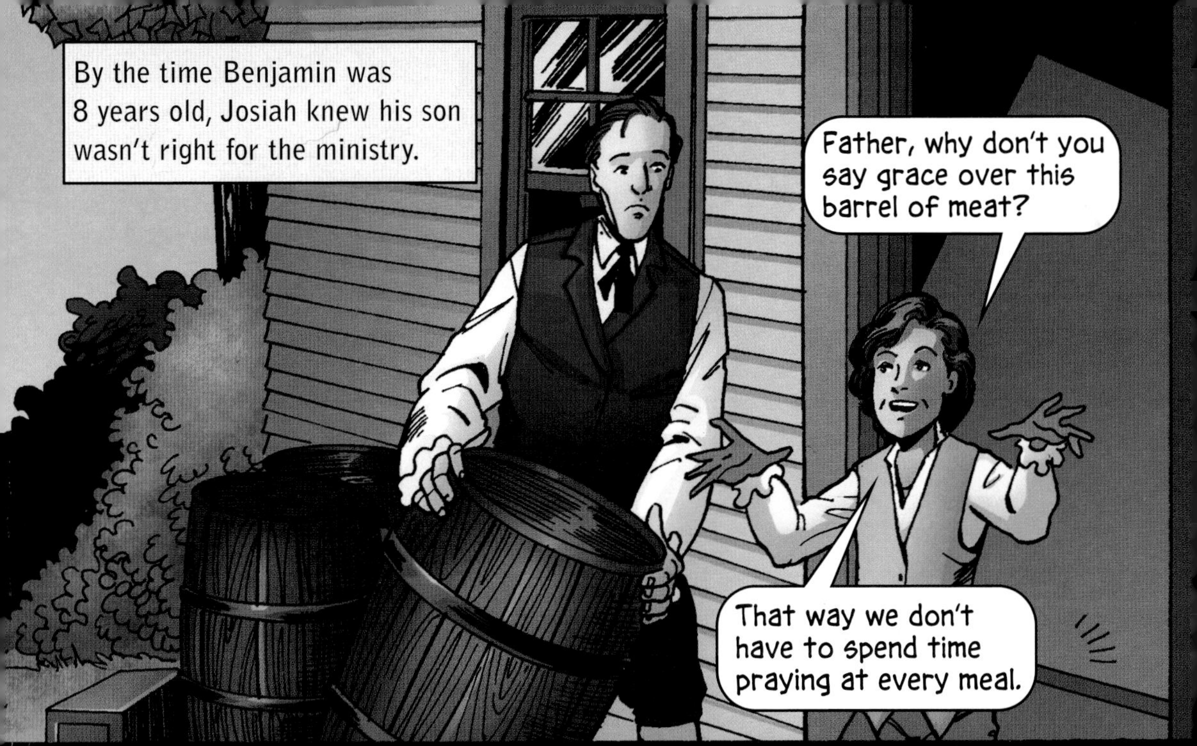
By the time Benjamin was 8 years old, Josiah knew his son wasn't right for the ministry.
Father, why don't you say grace over this barrel of meat?
That way we don't have to spend time praying at every meal.

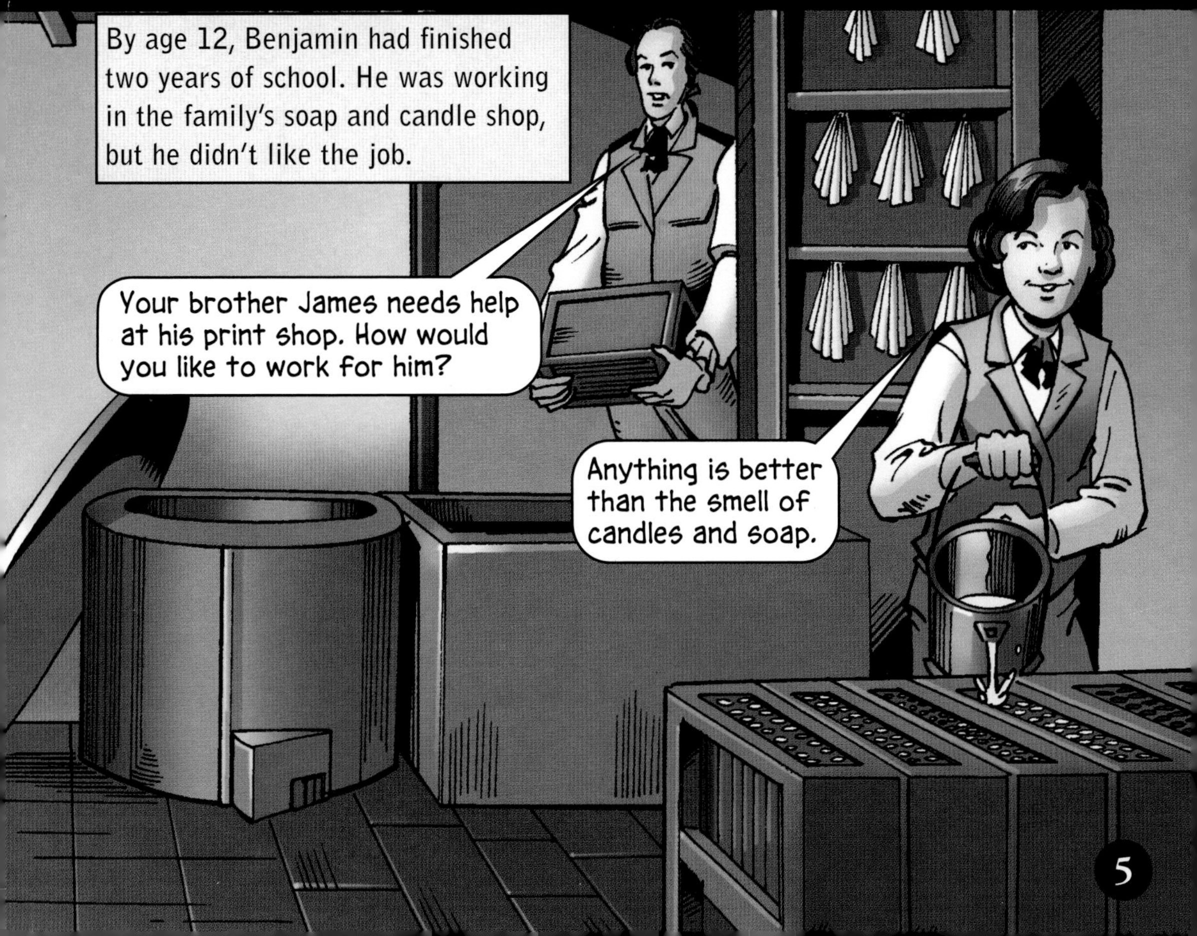
By age 12, Benjamin had finished two years of school. He was working in the family's soap and candle shop, but he didn't like the job.
Your brother James needs help at his print shop. How would you like to work for him?
Anything is better than the smell of candles and soap.

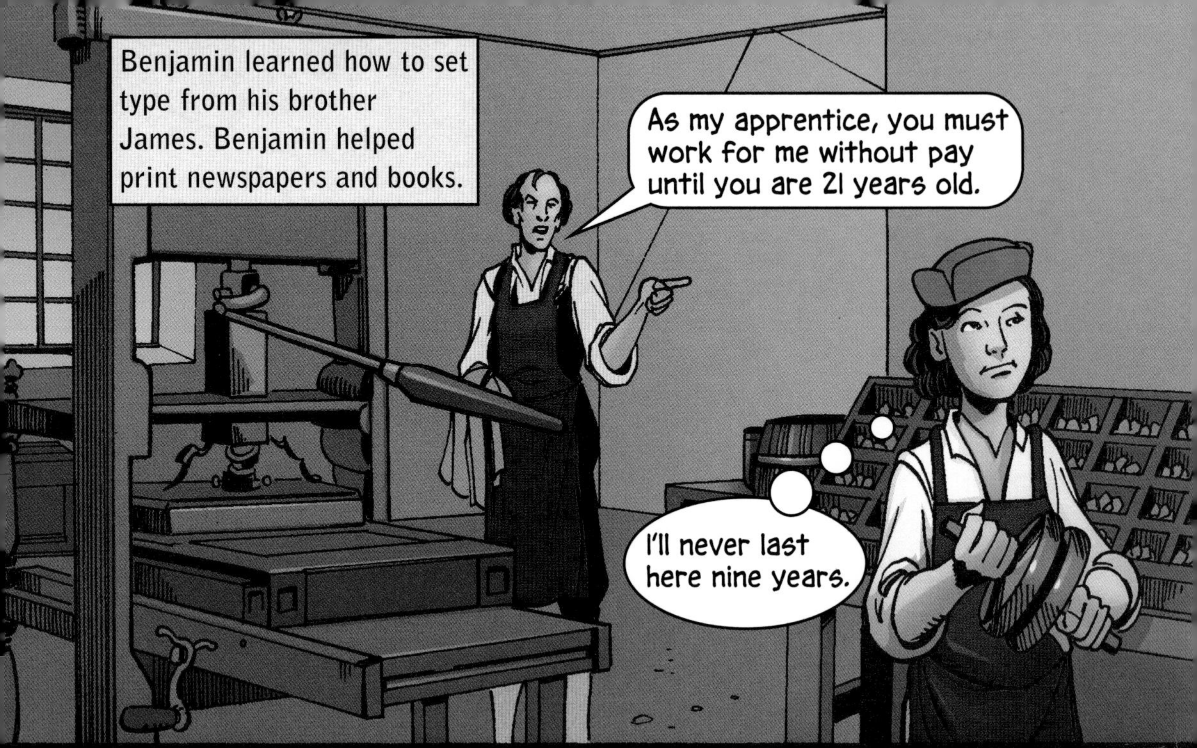
Benjamin learned how to set type from his brother James. Benjamin helped print newspapers and books.
As my apprentice, you must work for me without pay until you are 21 years old.
I'll never last here nine years.

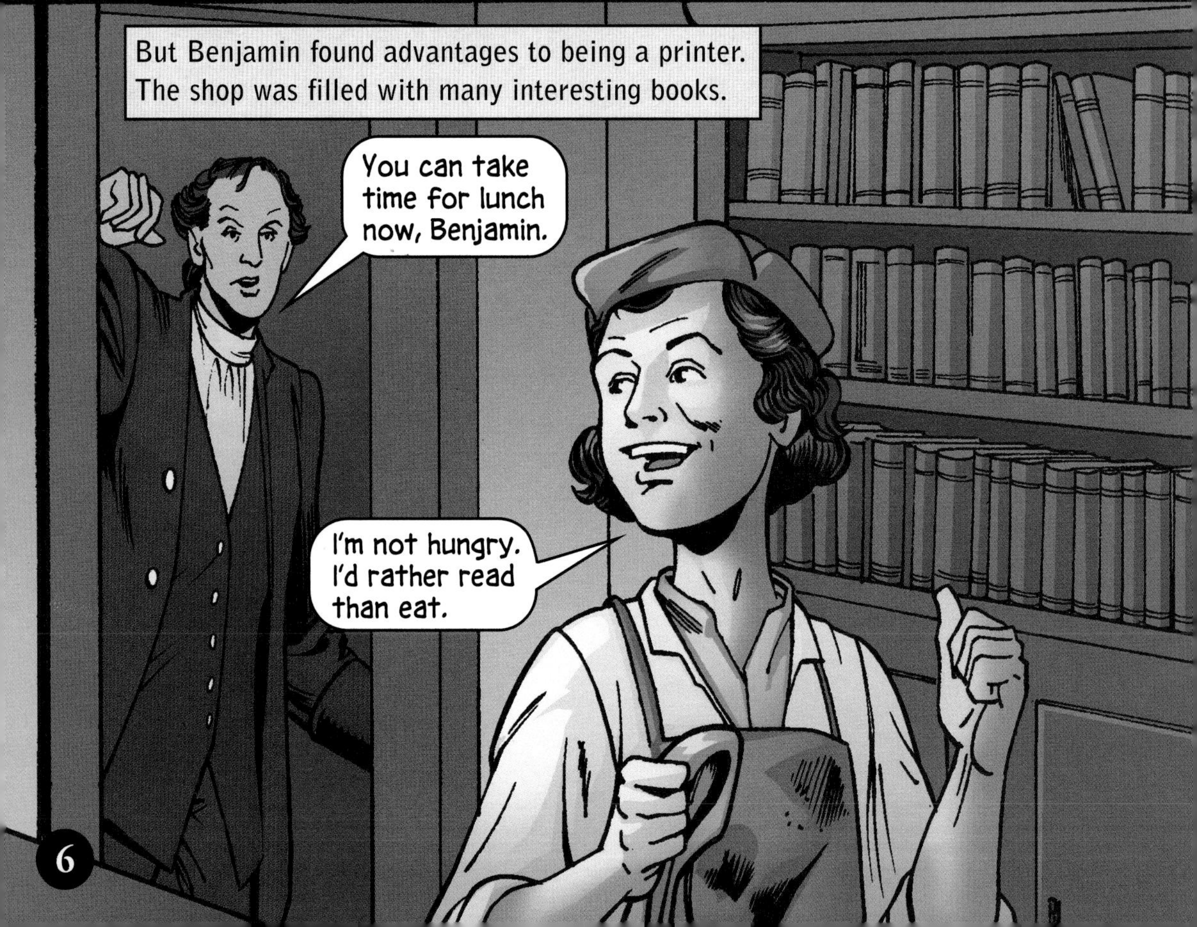
But Benjamin found advantages to being a printer. The shop was filled with many interesting books.
You can take time for lunch now, Benjamin.
I'm not hungry. I'd rather read than eat.

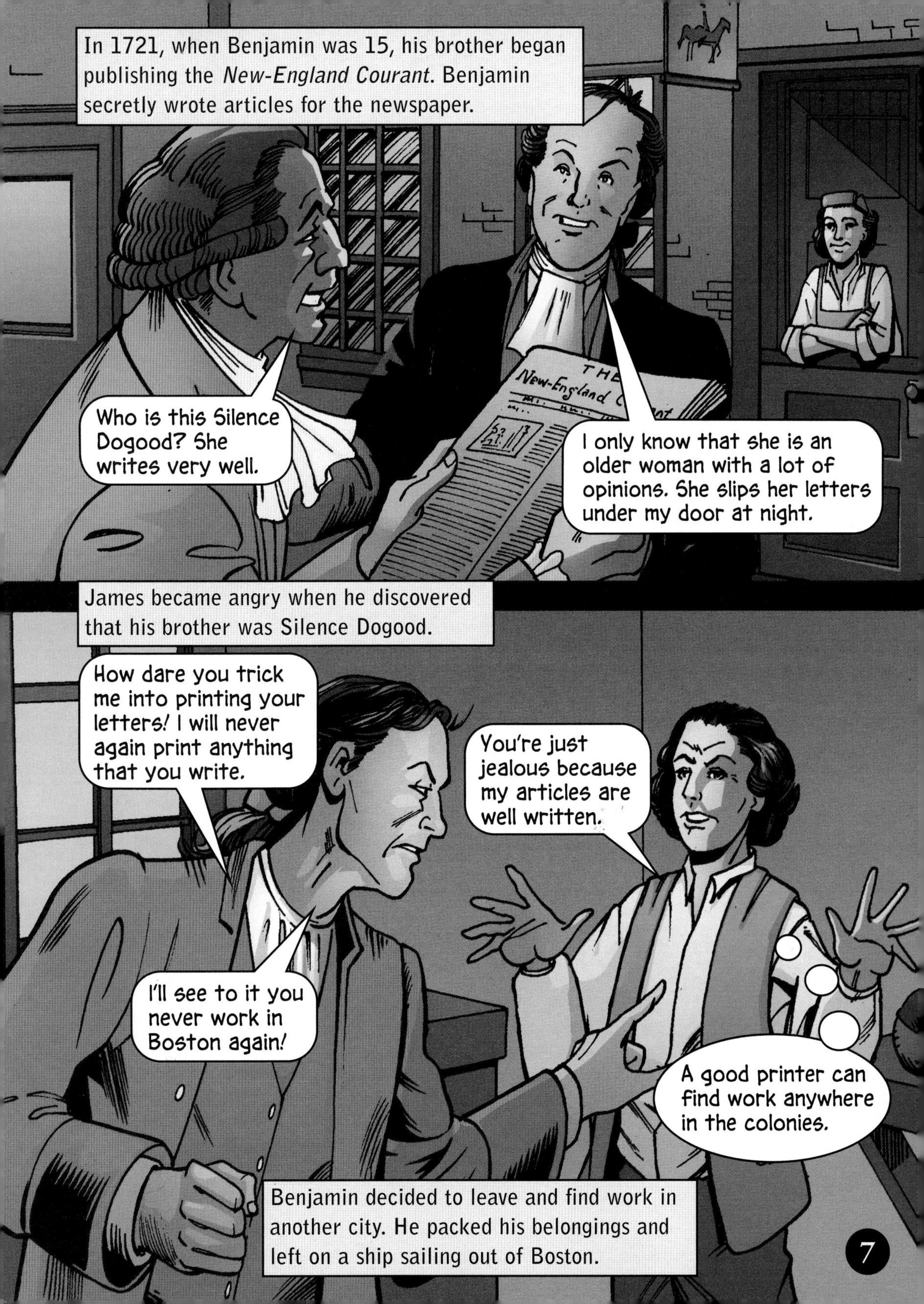
In 1721, when Benjamin was 15, his brother began publishing the *New-England Courant*. Benjamin secretly wrote articles for the newspaper.
Who is this Silence Dogood? She writes very well.
I only know that she is an older woman with a lot of opinions. She slips her letters under my door at night.
James became angry when he discovered that his brother was Silence Dogood.
How dare you trick me into printing your letters! I will never again print anything that you write.
You're just jealous because my articles are well written.
I'll see to it you never work in Boston again!
A good printer can find work anywhere in the colonies.
Benjamin decided to leave and find work in another city. He packed his belongings and left on a ship sailing out of Boston.

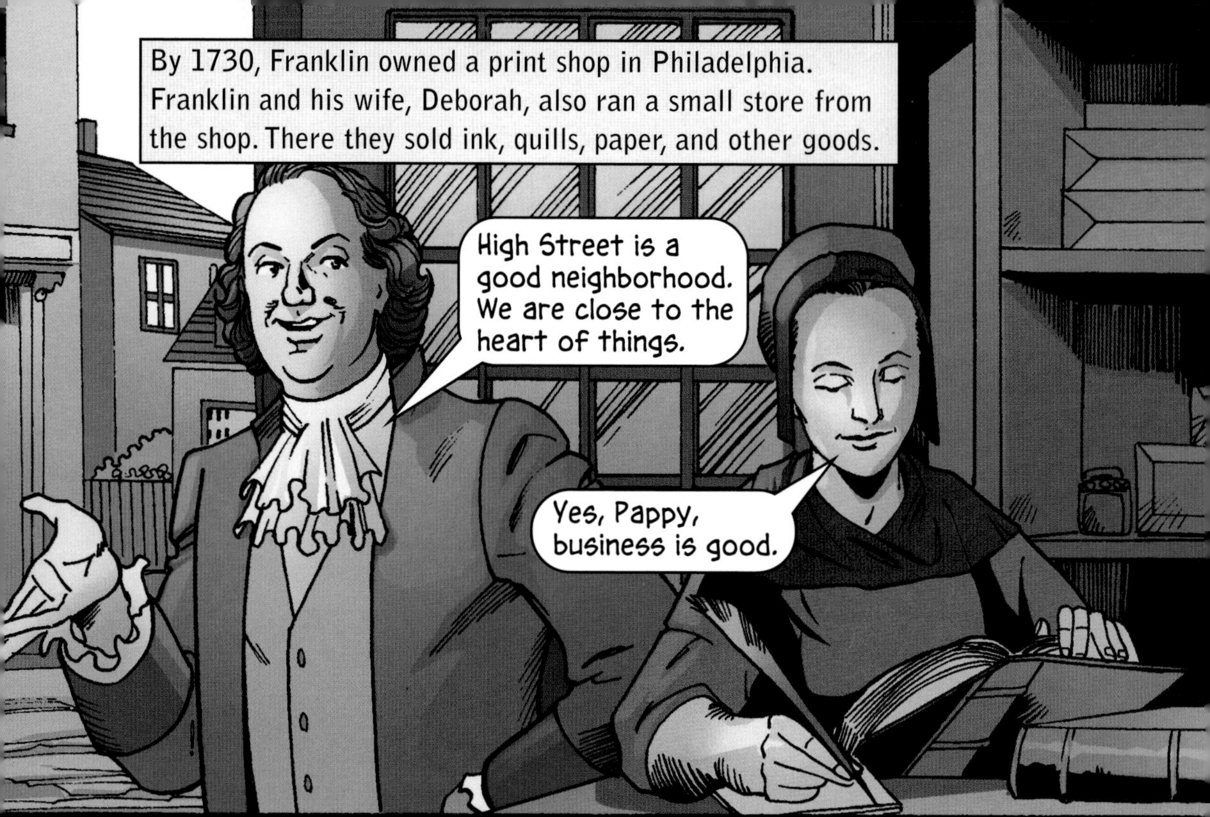
By 1730, Franklin owned a print shop in Philadelphia. Franklin and his wife, Deborah, also ran a small store from the shop. There they sold ink, quills, paper, and other goods.
High Street is a good neighborhood. We are close to the heart of things.
Yes, Pappy, business is good.

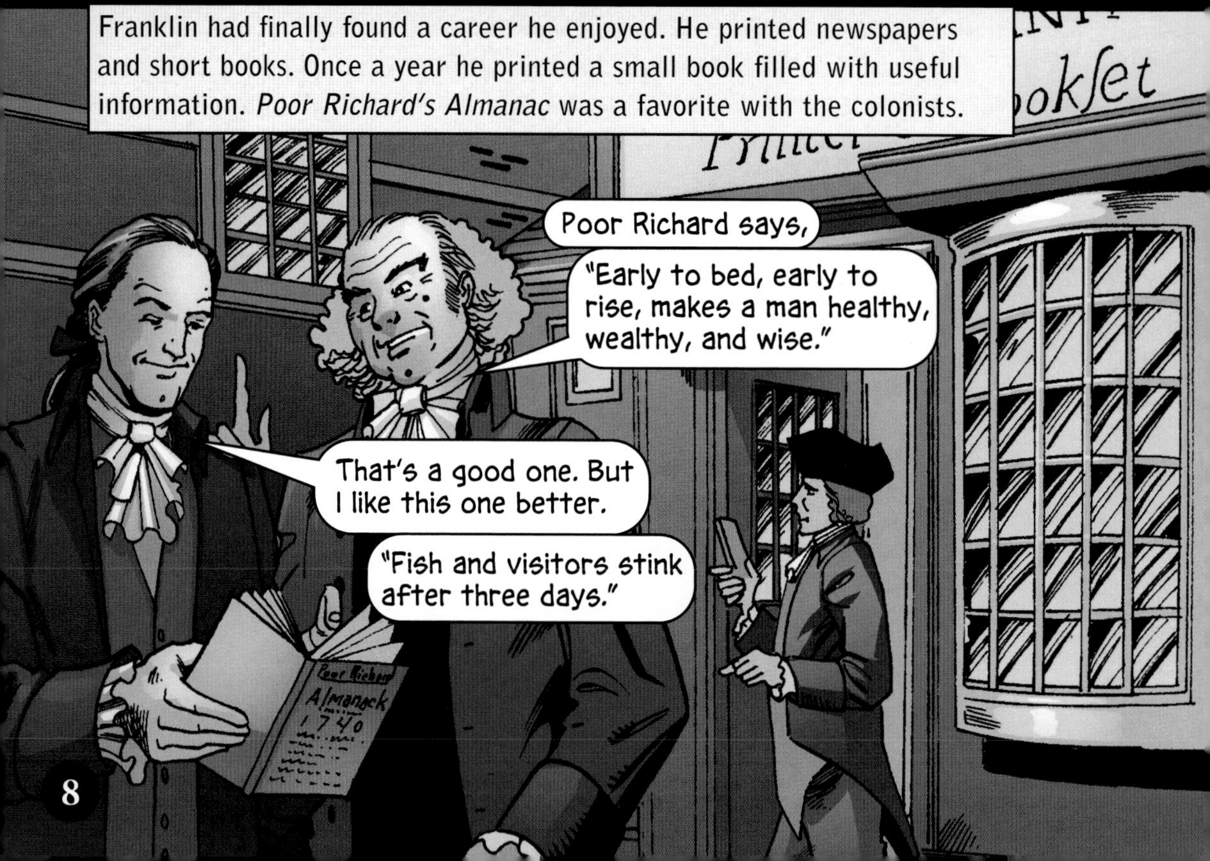
Franklin had finally found a career he enjoyed. He printed newspapers and short books. Once a year he printed a small book filled with useful information. *Poor Richard's Almanac* was a favorite with the colonists.
Poor Richard says,
"Early to bed, early to rise, makes a man healthy, wealthy, and wise."
That's a good one. But I like this one better.
"Fish and visitors stink after three days."

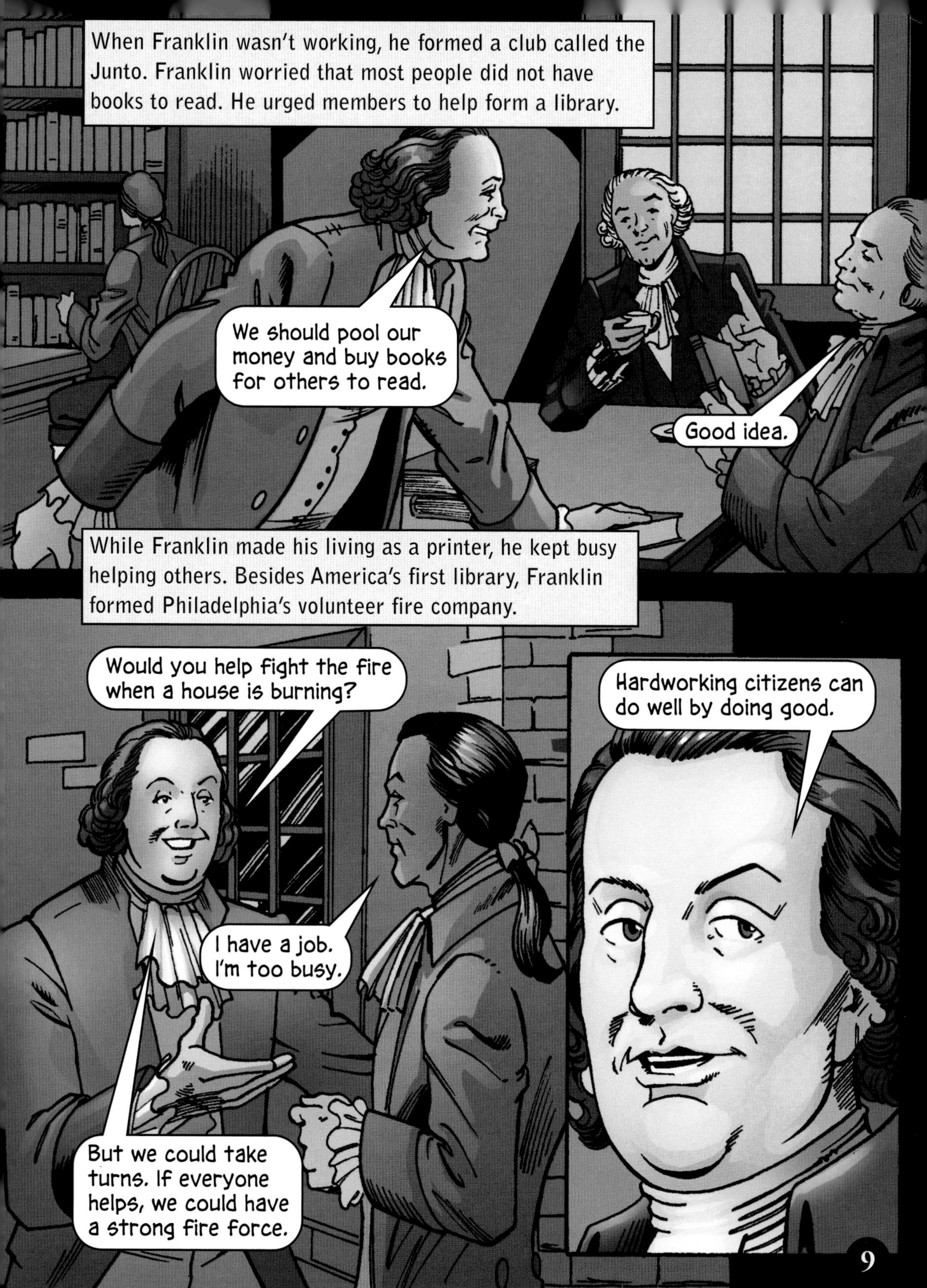
When Franklin wasn't working, he formed a club called the Junto. Franklin worried that most people did not have books to read. He urged members to help form a library.
We should pool our money and buy books for others to read.
Good idea.
While Franklin made his living as a printer, he kept busy helping others. Besides America's first library, Franklin formed Philadelphia's volunteer fire company.
Would you help fight the fire when a house is burning?
I have a job. I'm too busy.
But we could take turns. If everyone helps, we could have a strong fire force.
Hardworking citizens can do well by doing good.

Chapter 2
INVENTOR

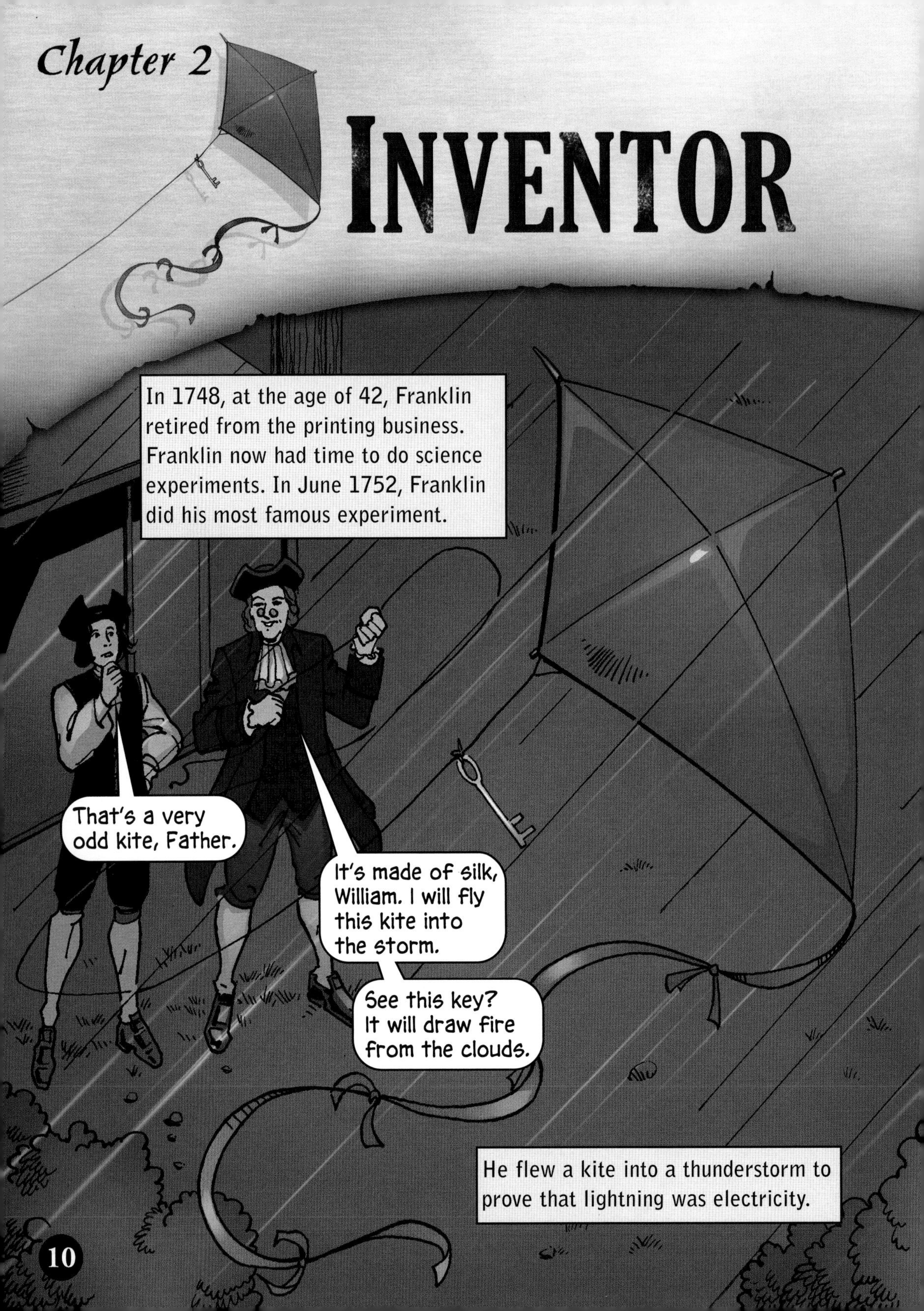
In 1748, at the age of 42, Franklin retired from the printing business. Franklin now had time to do science experiments. In June 1752, Franklin did his most famous experiment.
That's a very odd kite, Father.
It's made of silk, William. I will fly this kite into the storm.
See this key? It will draw fire from the clouds.
He flew a kite into a thunderstorm to prove that lightning was electricity.

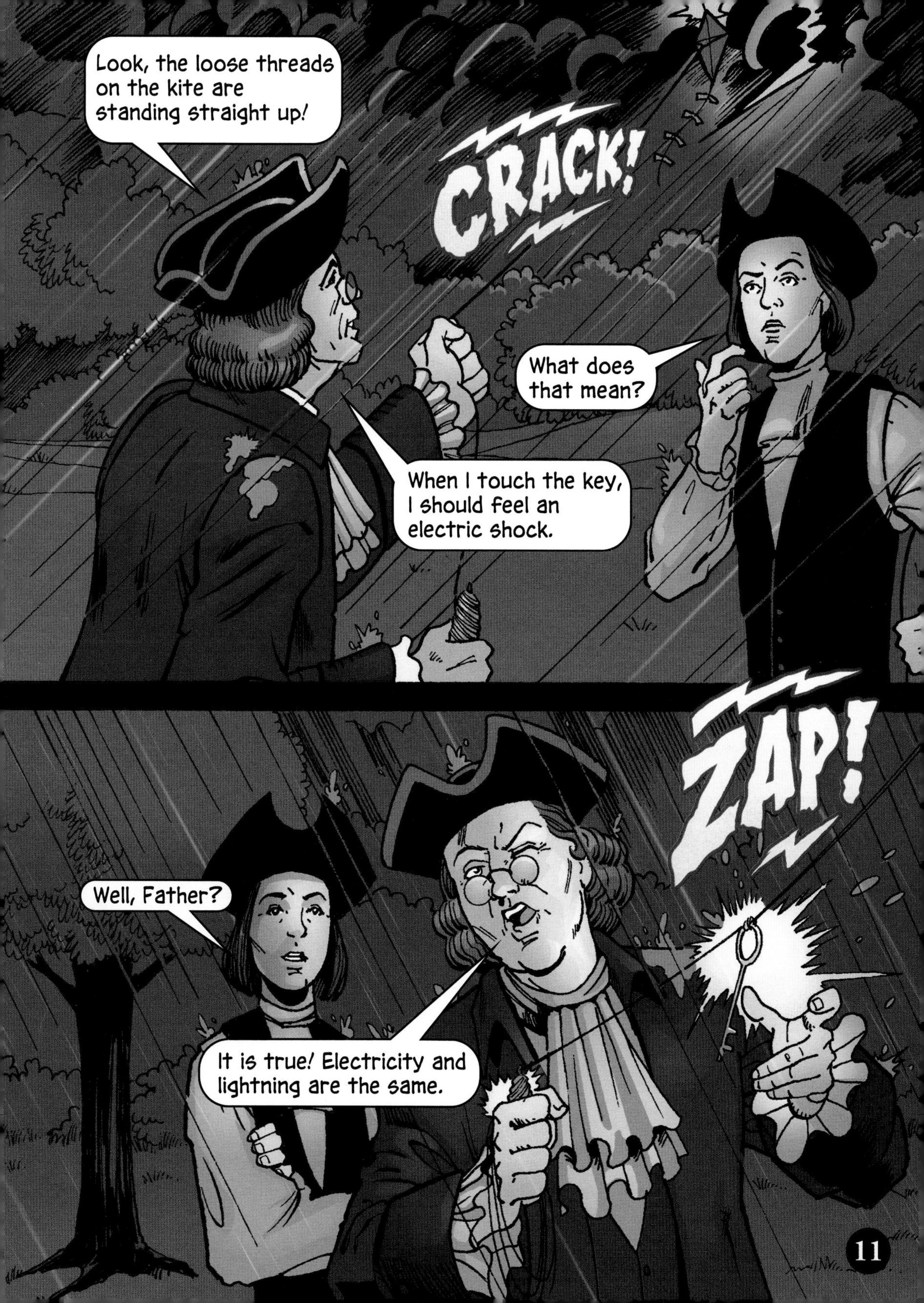
Look, the loose threads on the kite are standing straight up!
CRACK!
What does that mean?
When I touch the key, I should feel an electric shock.
ZAP!
Well, Father?
It is true! Electricity and lightning are the same.

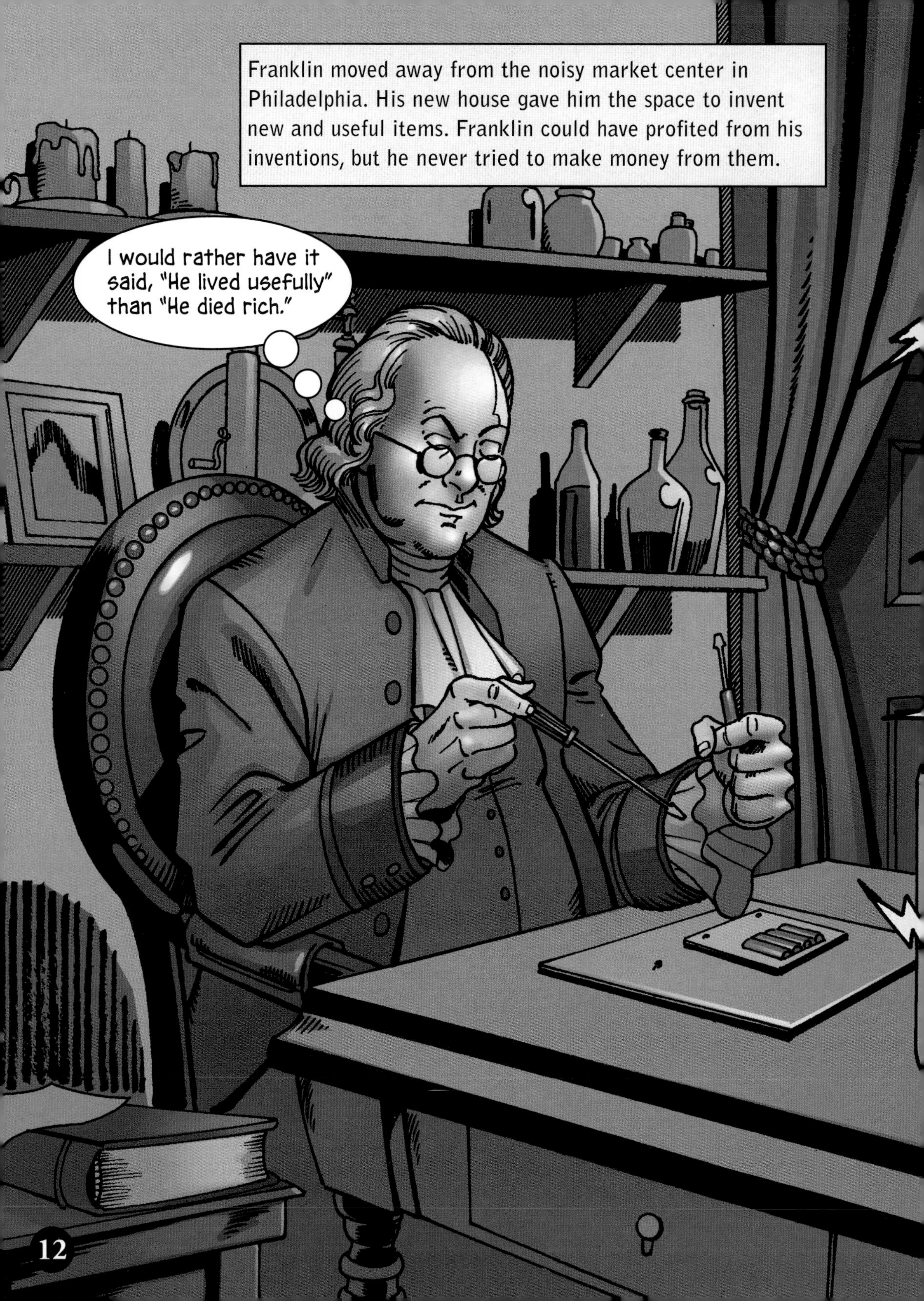
Franklin moved away from the noisy market center in Philadelphia. His new house gave him the space to invent new and useful items. Franklin could have profited from his inventions, but he never tried to make money from them.
I would rather have it said, "He lived usefully" than "He died rich."

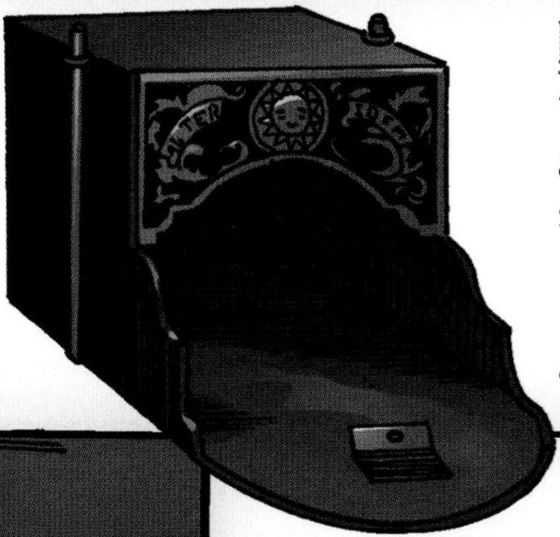

TER

Franklin Stove

This stove could heat a room without making smoke. First called a Pennsylvania Fireplace, it soon became known as the Franklin stove.

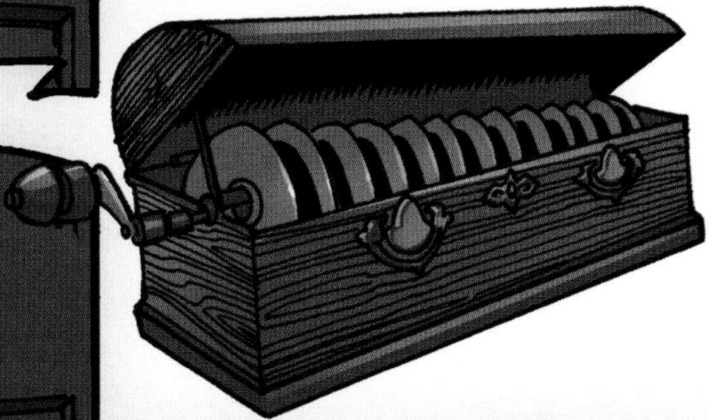

Armonica

Franklin invented a musical instrument called the glass armonica. It had a row of 27 glass jars of different sizes. To make music, people touched the spinning jars with wet fingers.

Lightning Rod

Lightning often struck colonial buildings, starting them on fire. Franklin asked the people of Philadelphia to put lighting rods on tall buildings. These lightning rods kept buildings from starting on fire.

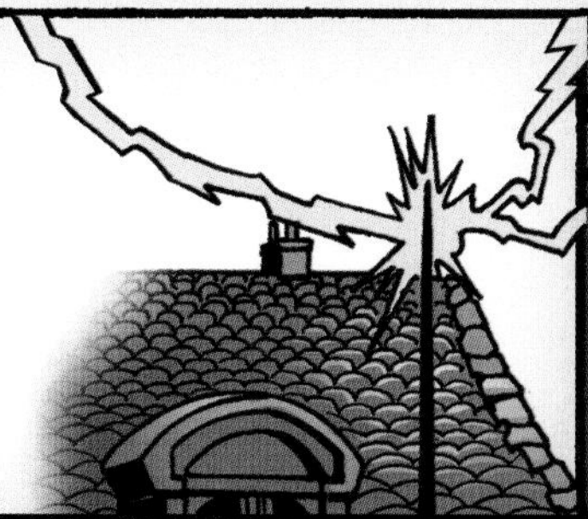

Bifocals

Franklin needed two pairs of glasses. He used one pair for reading and the other to see far away. He found it troublesome to switch pairs. He had a glass cutter cut both pairs of lenses in half. He glued the bottoms of one set to the tops of the other, inventing the bifocal lens.

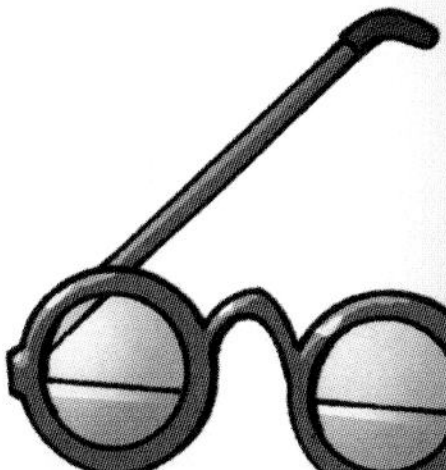

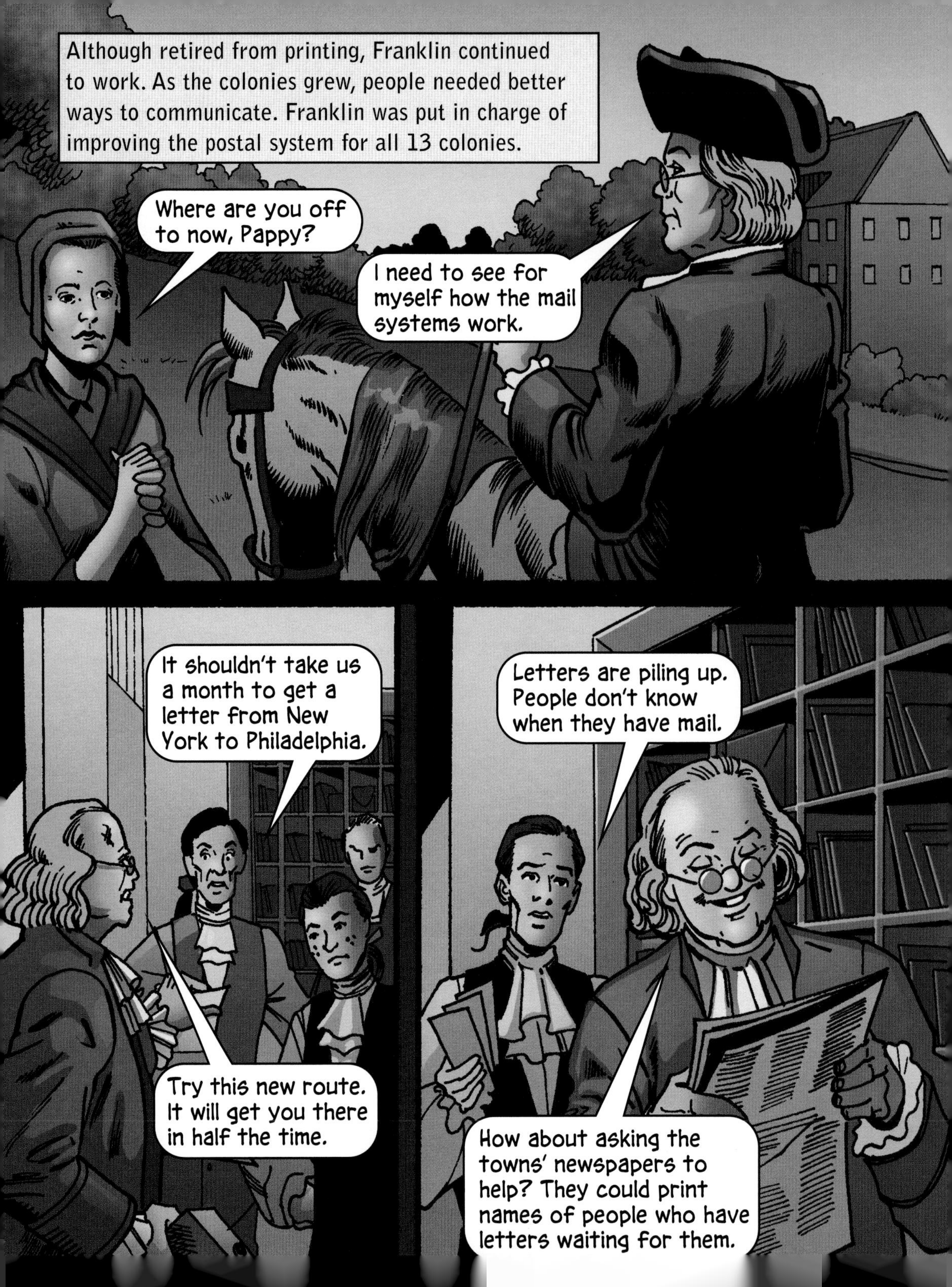
Although retired from printing, Franklin continued to work. As the colonies grew, people needed better ways to communicate. Franklin was put in charge of improving the postal system for all 13 colonies.
Where are you off to now, Pappy?
I need to see for myself how the mail systems work.
It shouldn't take us a month to get a letter from New York to Philadelphia.
Try this new route. It will get you there in half the time.
Letters are piling up. People don't know when they have mail.
How about asking the towns' newspapers to help? They could print names of people who have letters waiting for them.

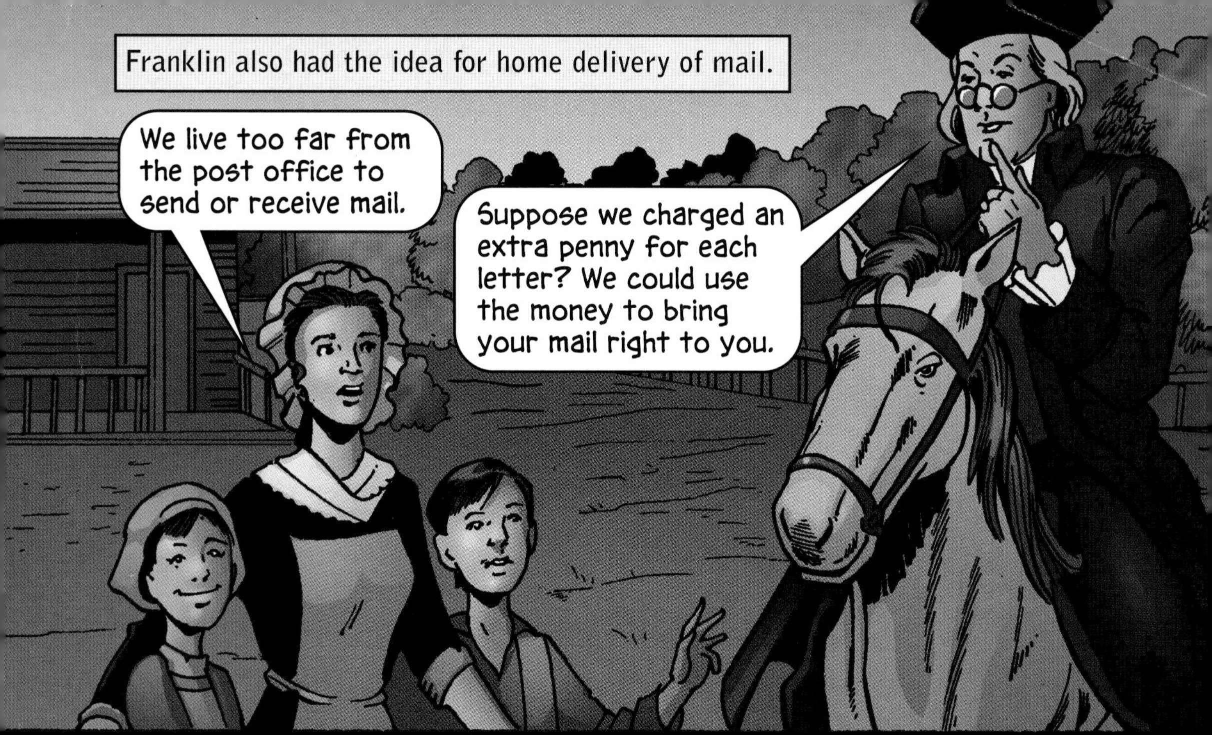
Franklin also had the idea for home delivery of mail.
We live too far from the post office to send or receive mail.
Suppose we charged an extra penny for each letter? We could use the money to bring your mail right to you.

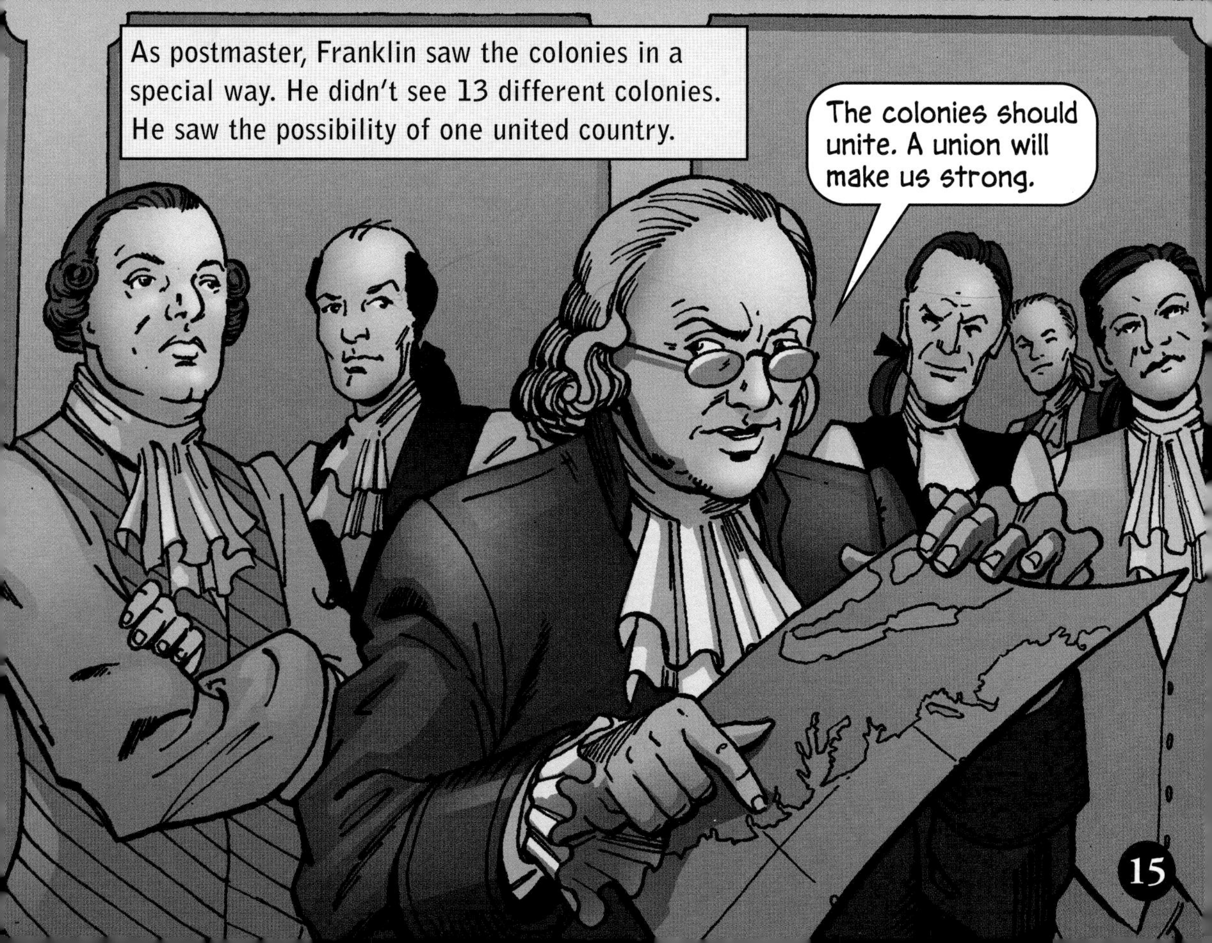
As postmaster, Franklin saw the colonies in a special way. He didn't see 13 different colonies. He saw the possibility of one united country.
The colonies should unite. A union will make us strong.

Chapter 3

PATRIOT

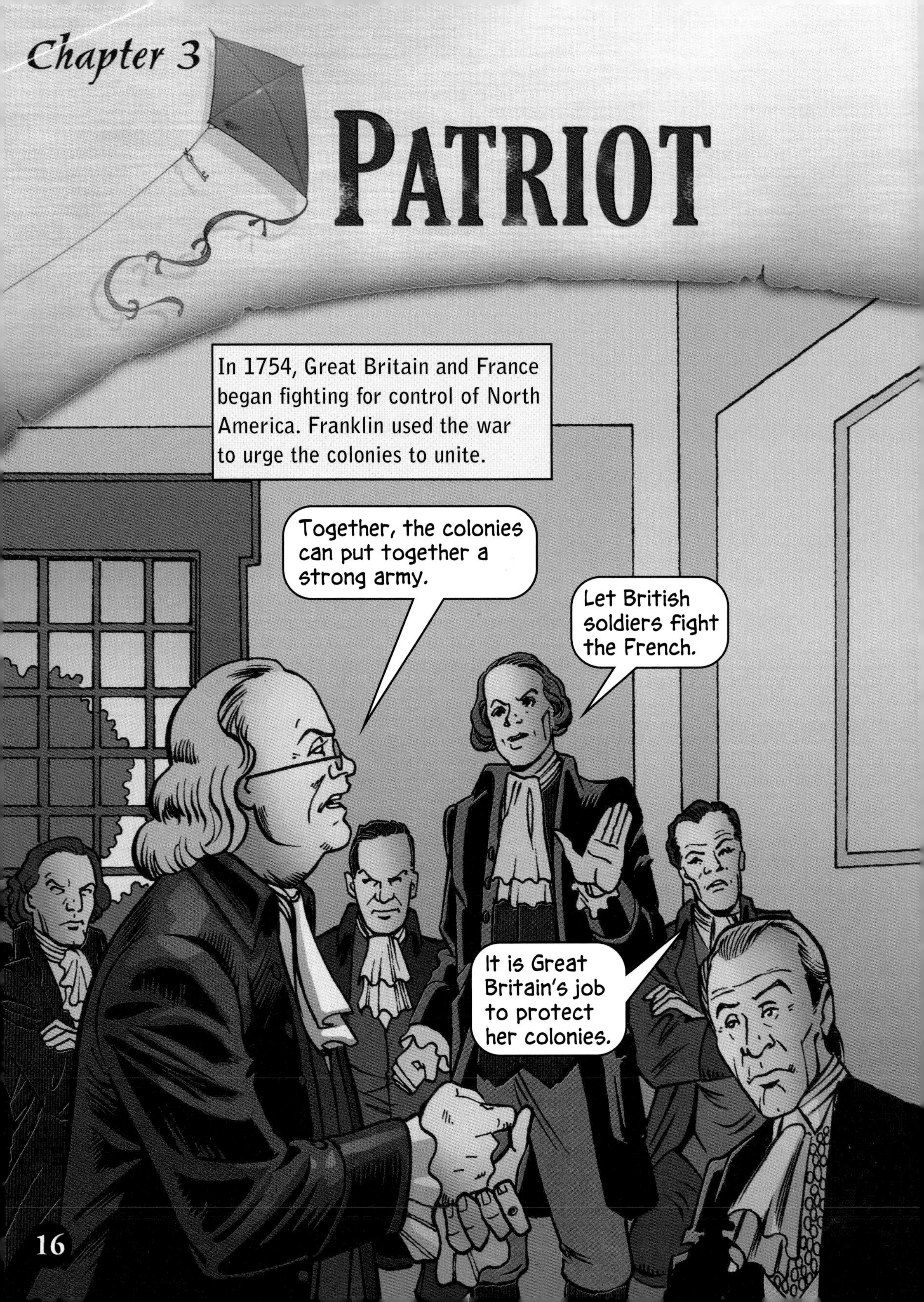
In 1754, Great Britain and France began fighting for control of North America. Franklin used the war to urge the colonies to unite.
Together, the colonies can put together a strong army.
Let British soldiers fight the French.
It is Great Britain's job to protect her colonies.

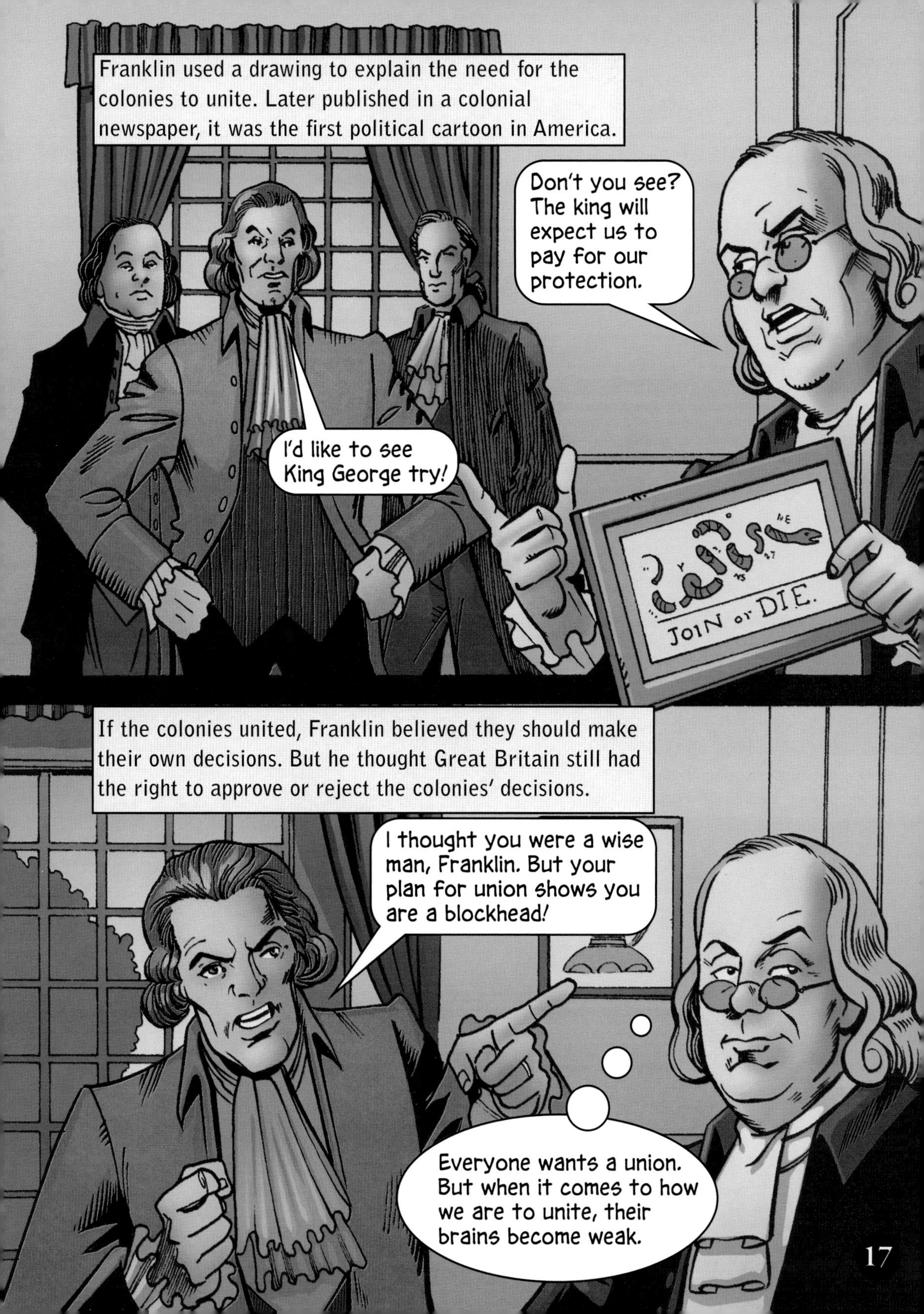
Franklin used a drawing to explain the need for the colonies to unite. Later published in a colonial newspaper, it was the first political cartoon in America.
Don't you see? The king will expect us to pay for our protection.
I'd like to see King George try!
JOIN or DIE.
If the colonies united, Franklin believed they should make their own decisions. But he thought Great Britain still had the right to approve or reject the colonies' decisions.
I thought you were a wise man, Franklin. But your plan for union shows you are a blockhead!
Everyone wants a union. But when it comes to how we are to unite, their brains become weak.

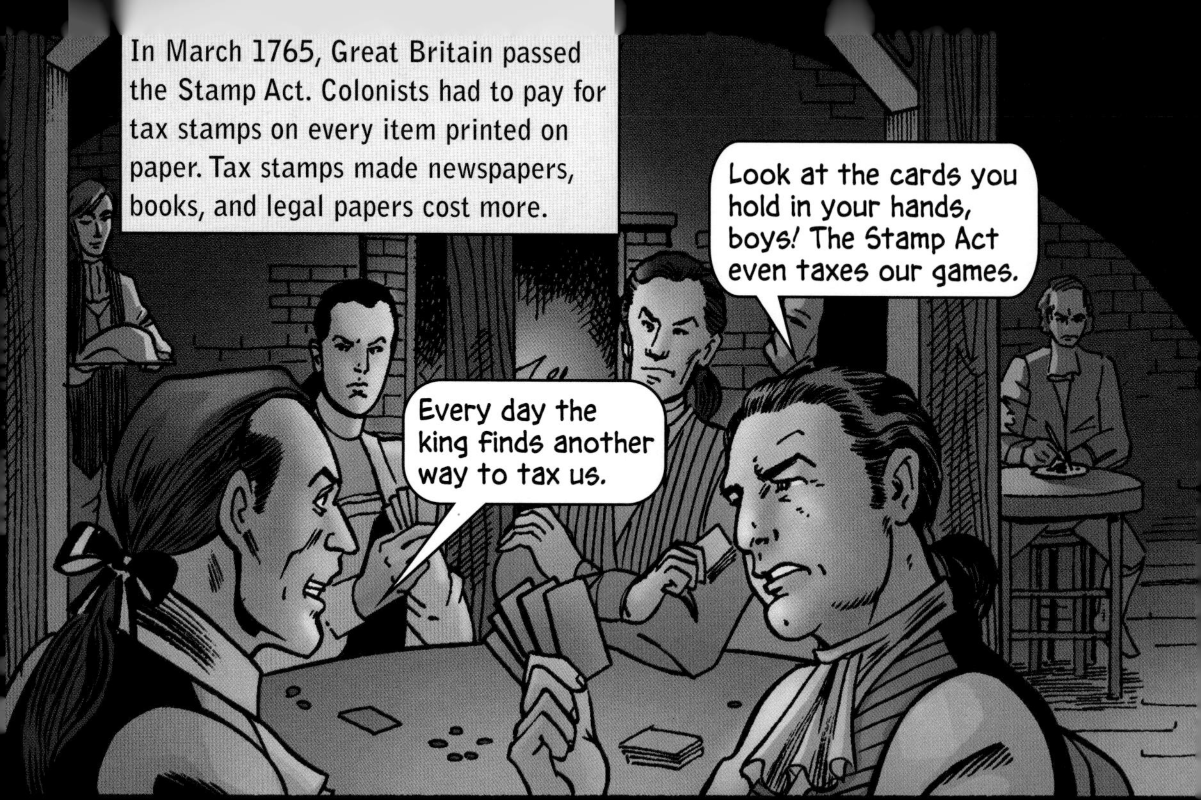
In March 1765, Great Britain passed the Stamp Act. Colonists had to pay for tax stamps on every item printed on paper. Tax stamps made newspapers, books, and legal papers cost more.
Look at the cards you hold in your hands, boys! The Stamp Act even taxes our games.
Every day the king finds another way to tax us.

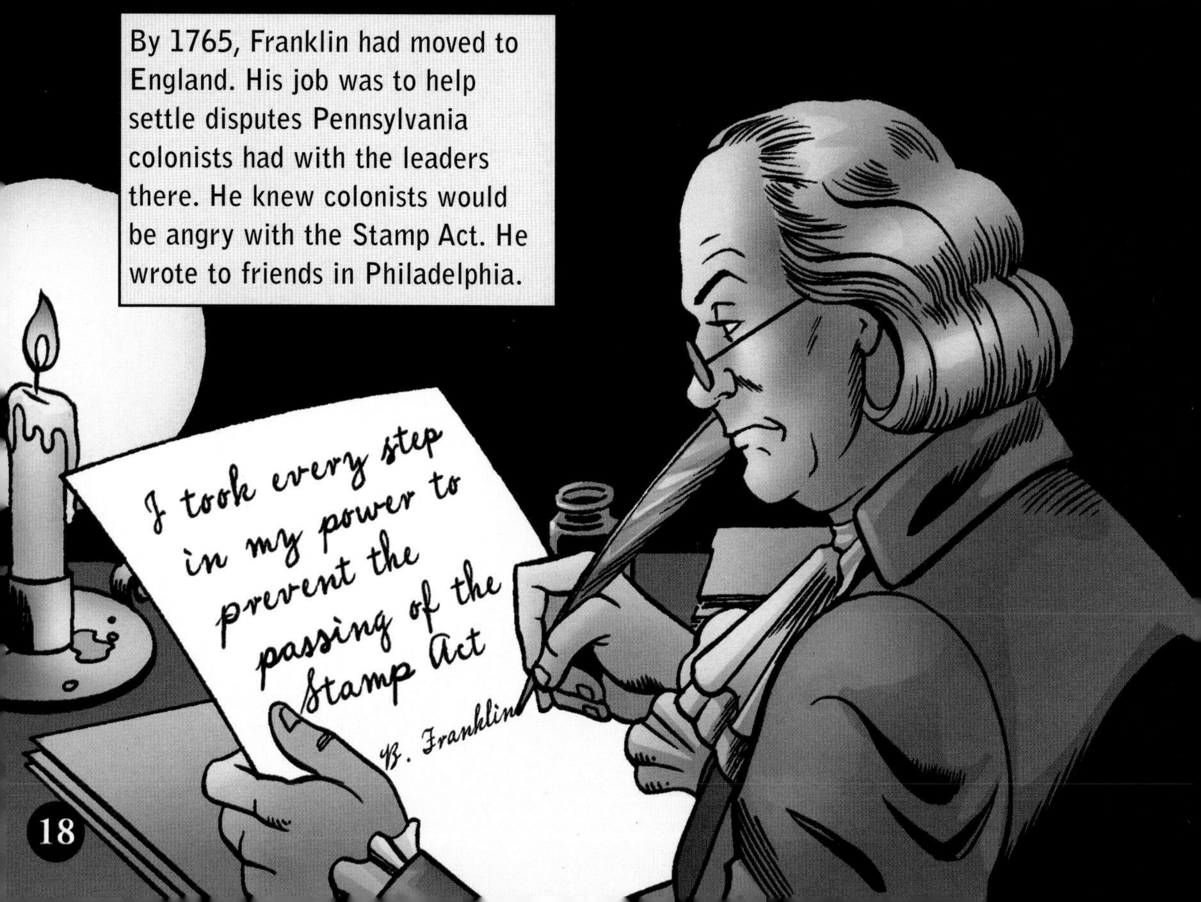
By 1765, Franklin had moved to England. His job was to help settle disputes Pennsylvania colonists had with the leaders there. He knew colonists would be angry with the Stamp Act. He wrote to friends in Philadelphia.
I took every step in my power to prevent the passing of the Stamp Act
B. Franklin

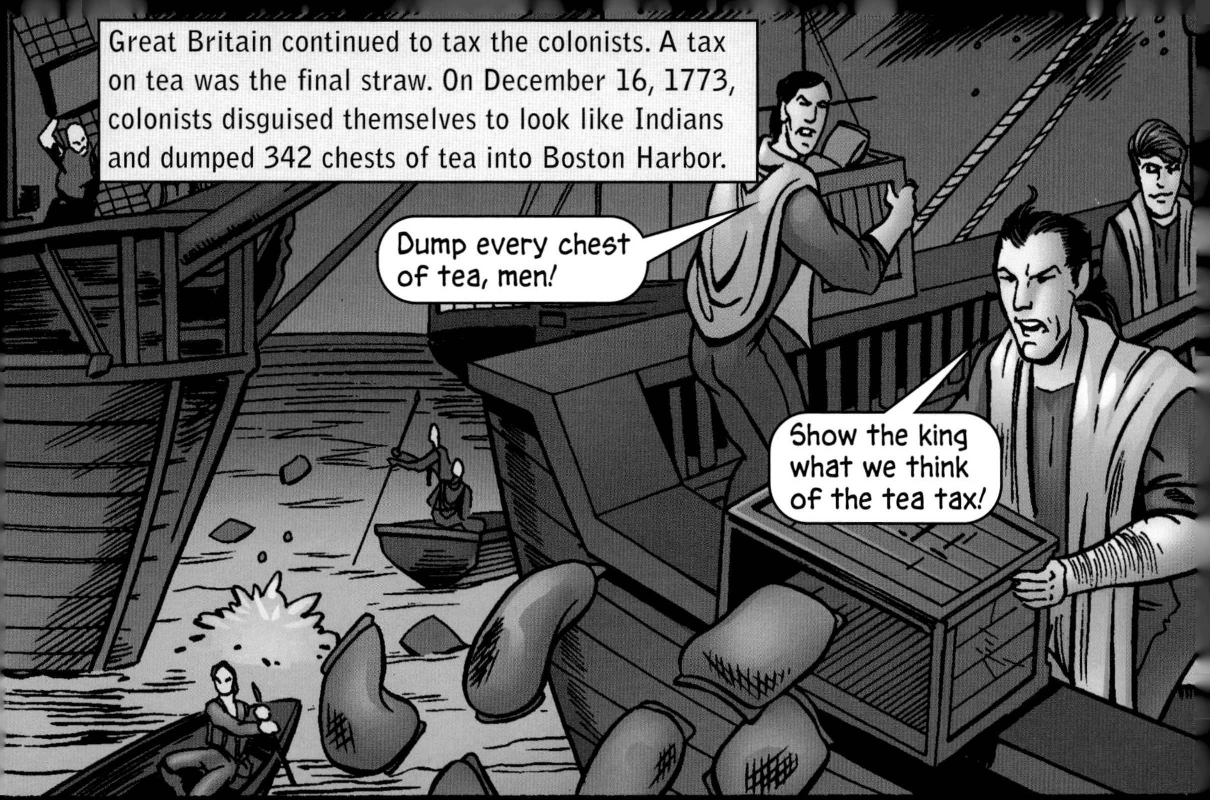
Great Britain continued to tax the colonists. A tax on tea was the final straw. On December 16, 1773, colonists disguised themselves to look like Indians and dumped 342 chests of tea into Boston Harbor.
Dump every chest of tea, men!
Show the king what we think of the tea tax!

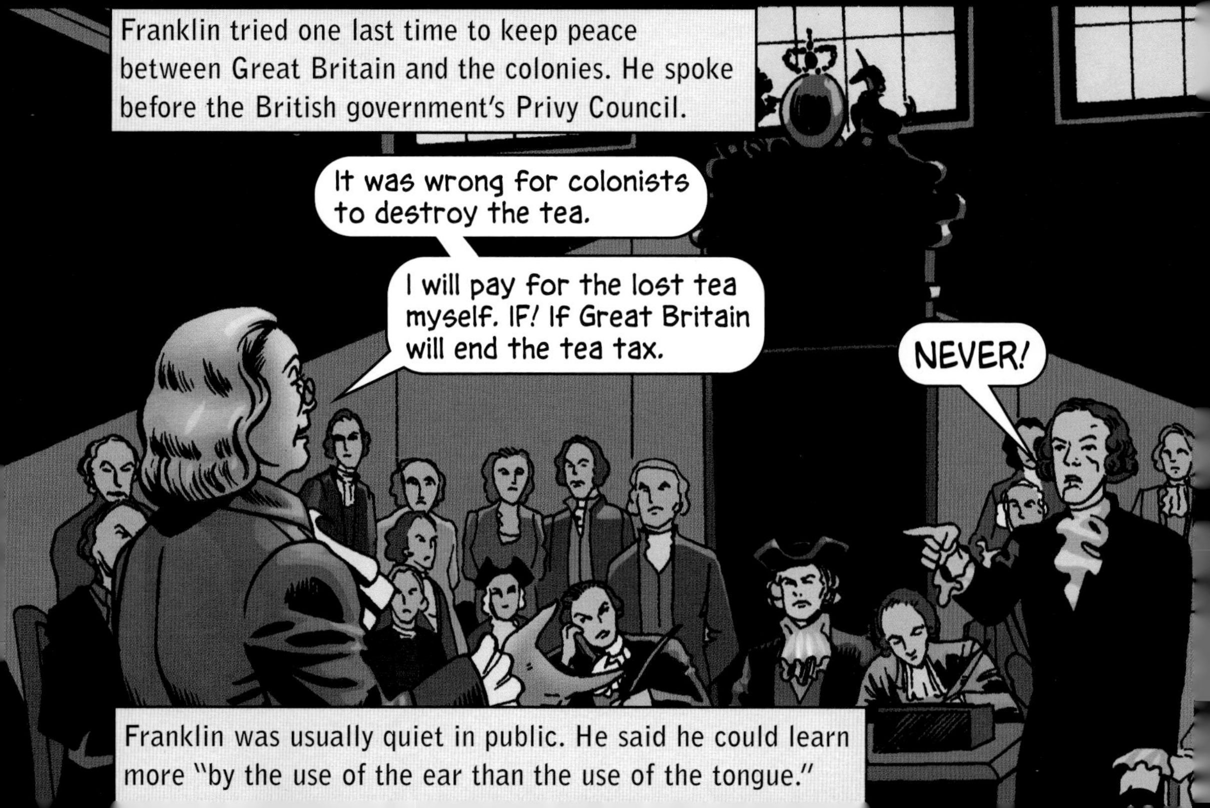
Franklin tried one last time to keep peace between Great Britain and the colonies. He spoke before the British government's Privy Council.
It was wrong for colonists to destroy the tea.
I will pay for the lost tea myself. IF! If Great Britain will end the tea tax.
NEVER!
Franklin was usually quiet in public. He said he could learn more "by the use of the ear than the use of the tongue."

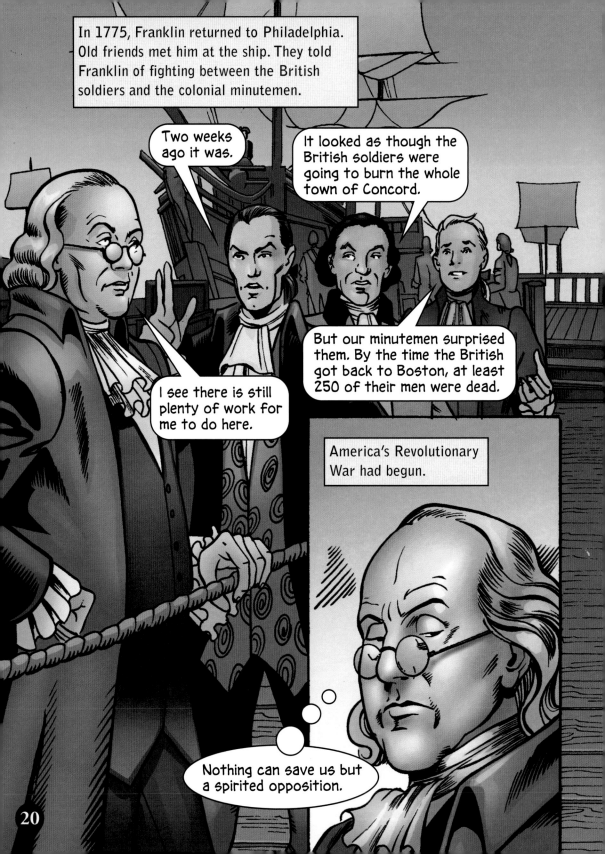

In 1775, Franklin returned to Philadelphia. Old friends met him at the ship. They told Franklin of fighting between the British soldiers and the colonial minutemen.

Two weeks ago it was.

It looked as though the British soldiers were going to burn the whole town of Concord.

I see there is still plenty of work for me to do here.

But our minutemen surprised them. By the time the British got back to Boston, at least 250 of their men were dead.

America's Revolutionary War had begun.

Nothing can save us but a spirited opposition.

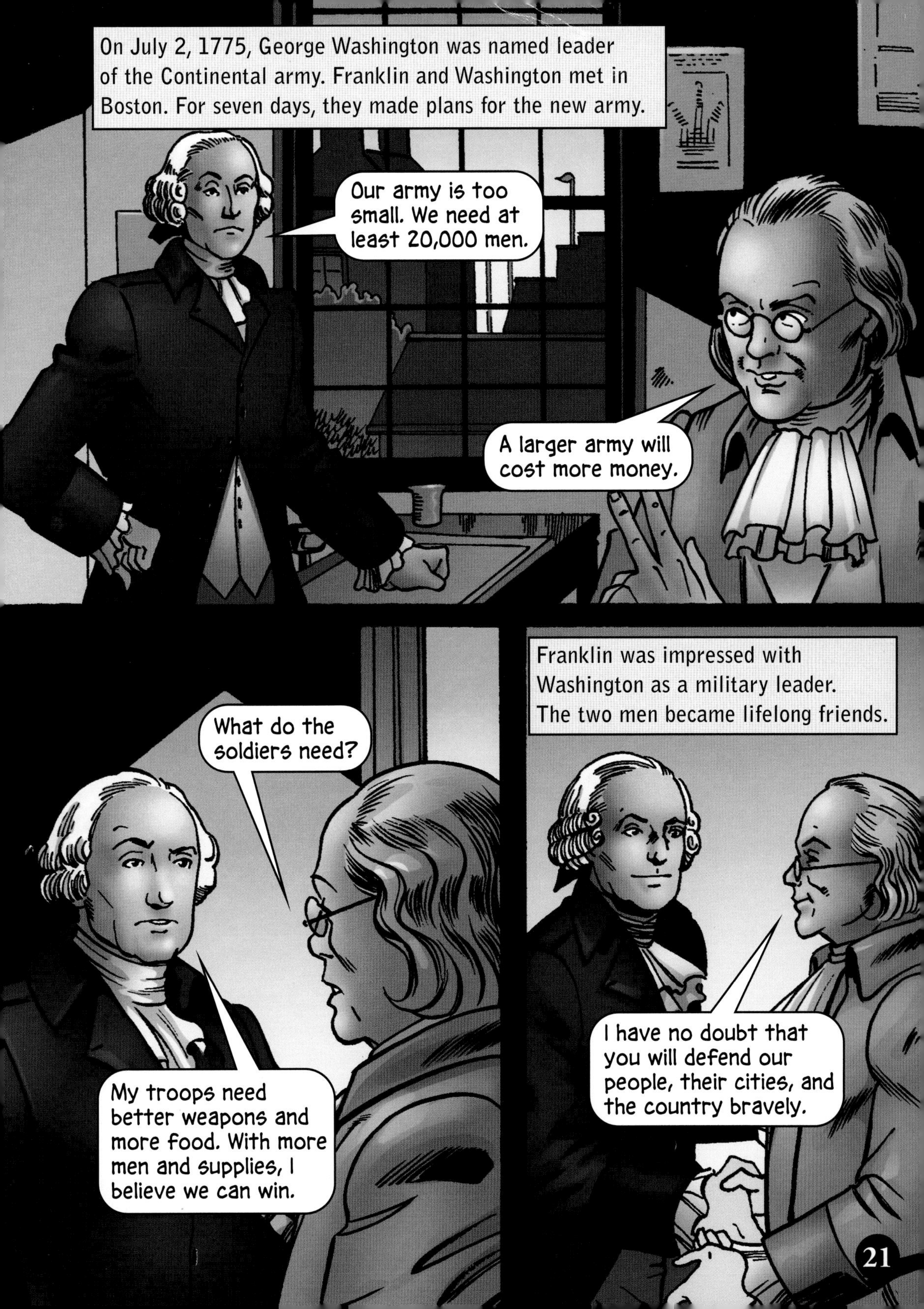
On July 2, 1775, George Washington was named leader of the Continental army. Franklin and Washington met in Boston. For seven days, they made plans for the new army.
Our army is too small. We need at least 20,000 men.
A larger army will cost more money.
What do the soldiers need?
My troops need better weapons and more food. With more men and supplies, I believe we can win.
Franklin was impressed with Washington as a military leader. The two men became lifelong friends.
I have no doubt that you will defend our people, their cities, and the country bravely.

Chapter 4

STATESMAN

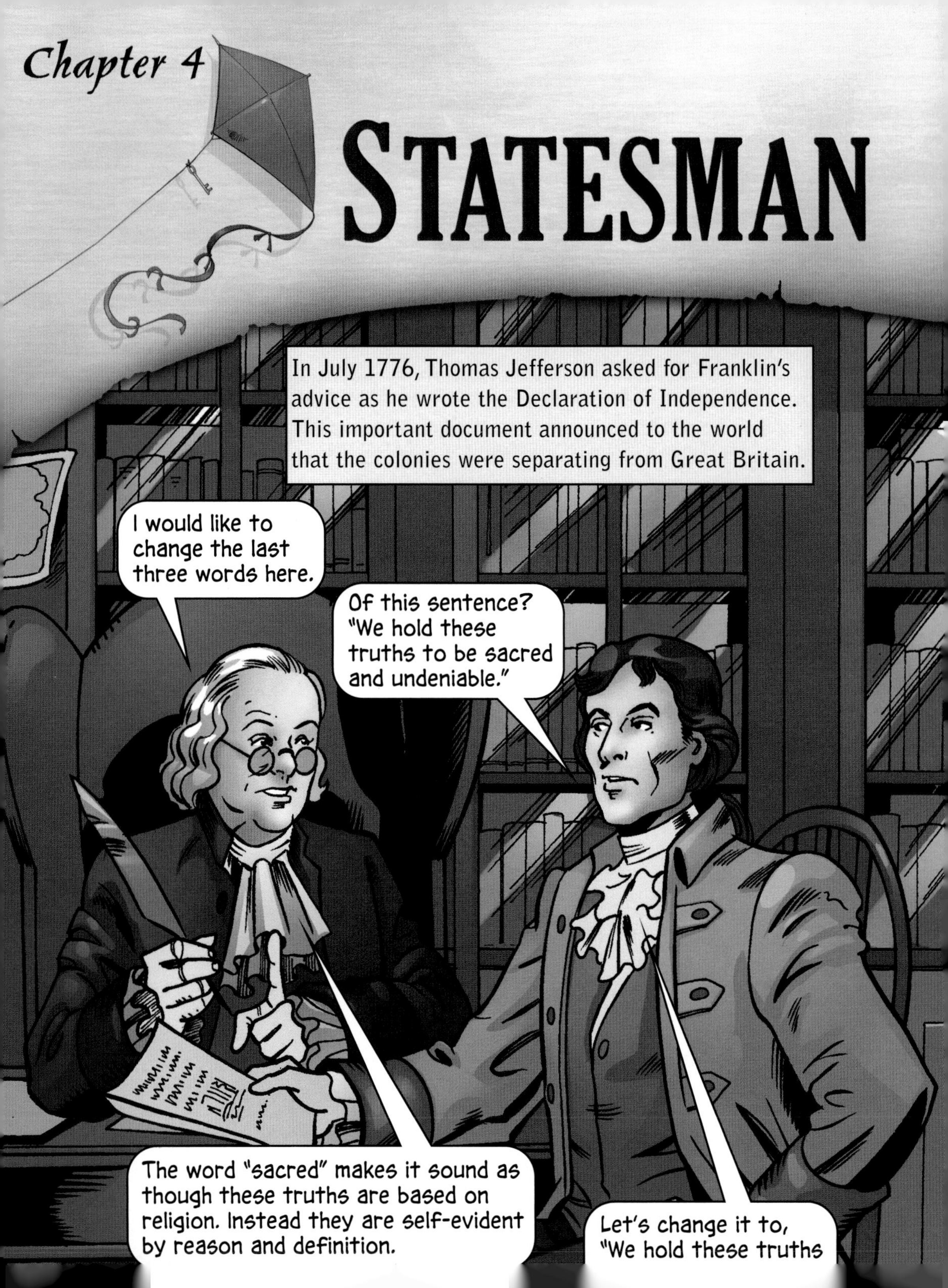

In July 1776, Thomas Jefferson asked for Franklin's advice as he wrote the Declaration of Independence. This important document announced to the world that the colonies were separating from Great Britain.
I would like to change the last three words here.
Of this sentence? "We hold these truths to be sacred and undeniable."
The word "sacred" makes it sound as though these truths are based on religion. Instead they are self-evident by reason and definition.
Let's change it to, "We hold these truths

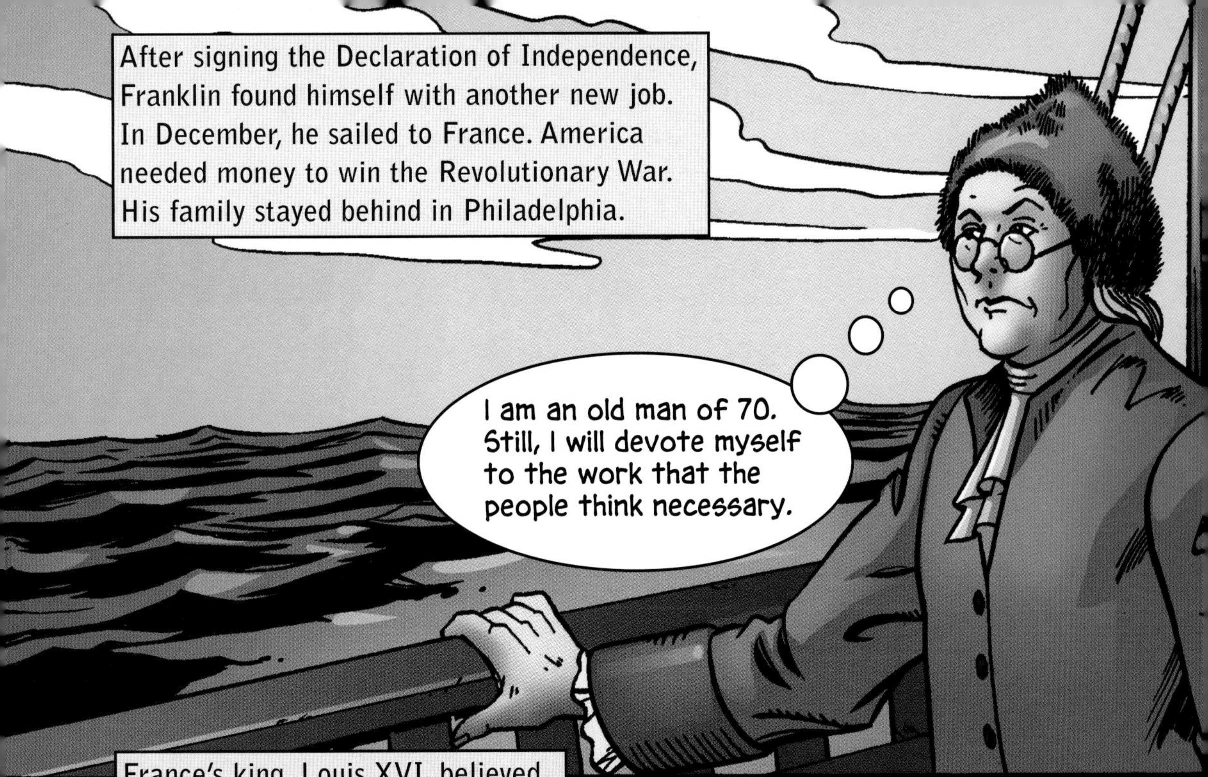
After signing the Declaration of Independence, Franklin found himself with another new job. In December, he sailed to France. America needed money to win the Revolutionary War. His family stayed behind in Philadelphia.
I am an old man of 70. Still, I will devote myself to the work that the people think necessary.

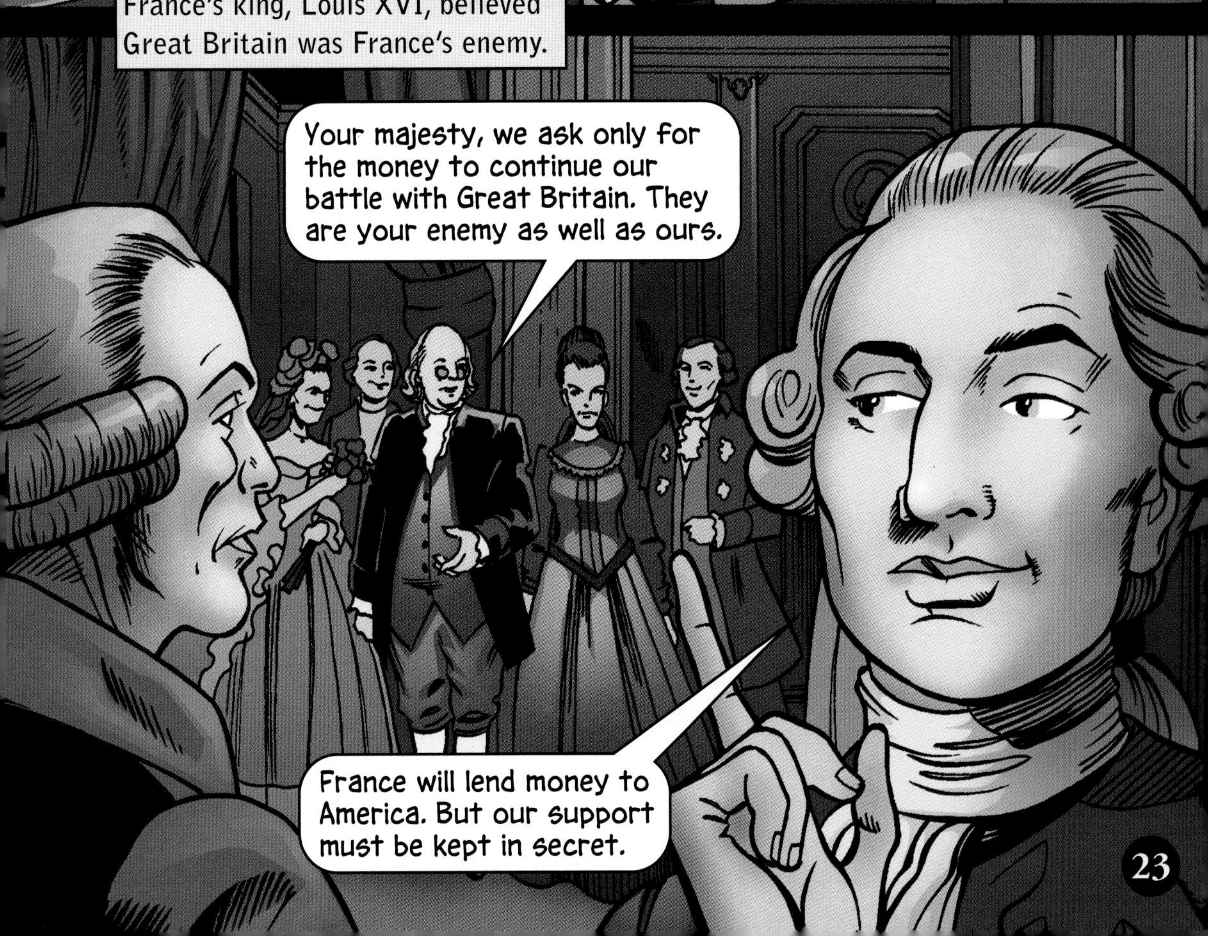
France's king, Louis XVI, believed Great Britain was France's enemy.
Your majesty, we ask only for the money to continue our battle with Great Britain. They are your enemy as well as ours.
France will lend money to America. But our support must be kept in secret.

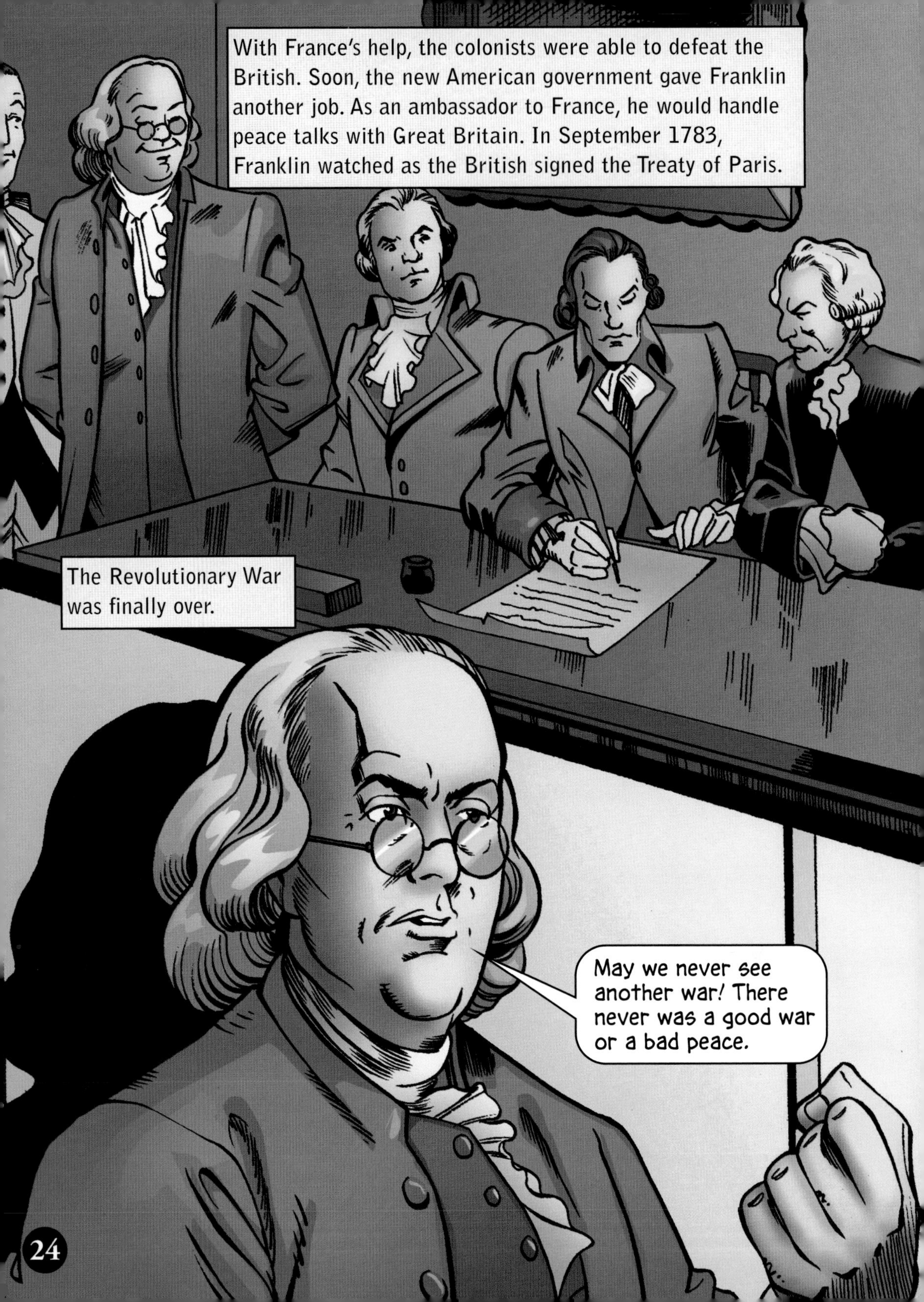
With France's help, the colonists were able to defeat the British. Soon, the new American government gave Franklin another job. As an ambassador to France, he would handle peace talks with Great Britain. In September 1783, Franklin watched as the British signed the Treaty of Paris.
The Revolutionary War was finally over.
May we never see another war! There never was a good war or a bad peace.

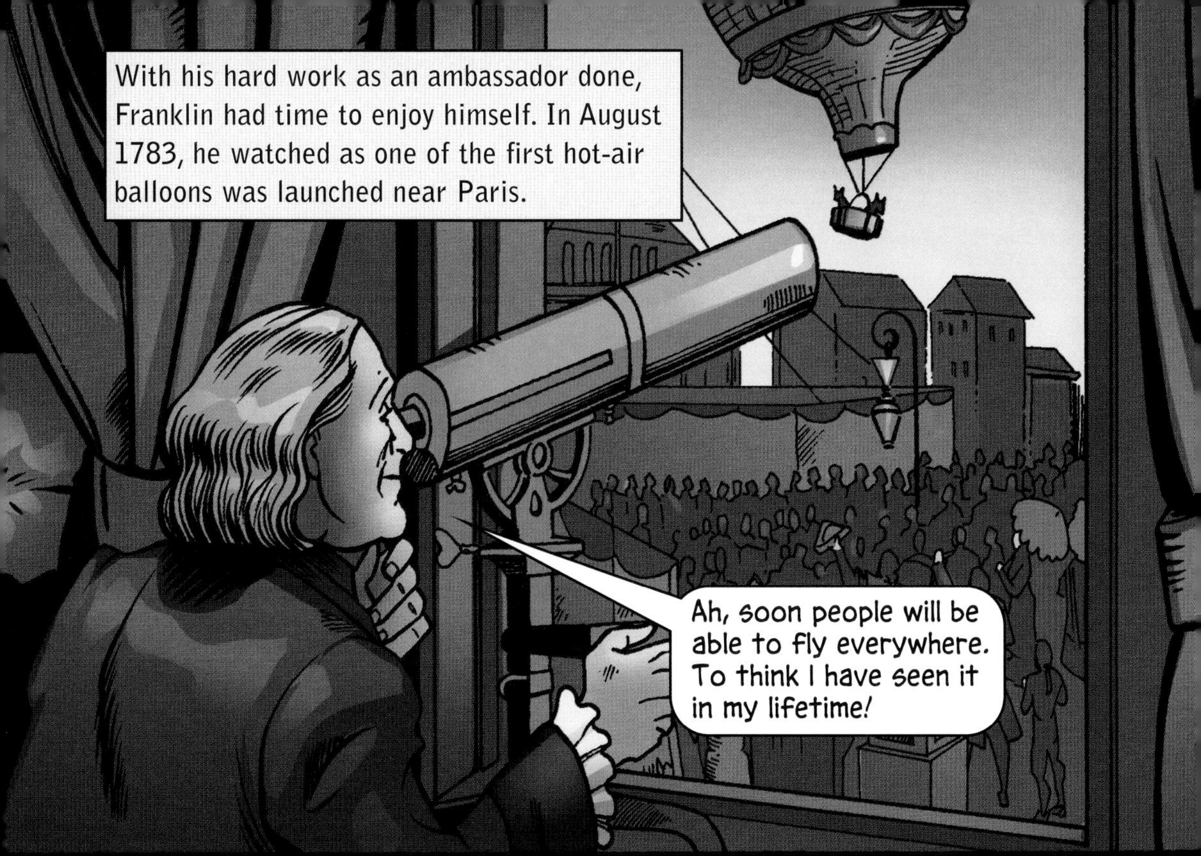
With his hard work as an ambassador done, Franklin had time to enjoy himself. In August 1783, he watched as one of the first hot-air balloons was launched near Paris.
Ah, soon people will be able to fly everywhere. To think I have seen it in my lifetime!

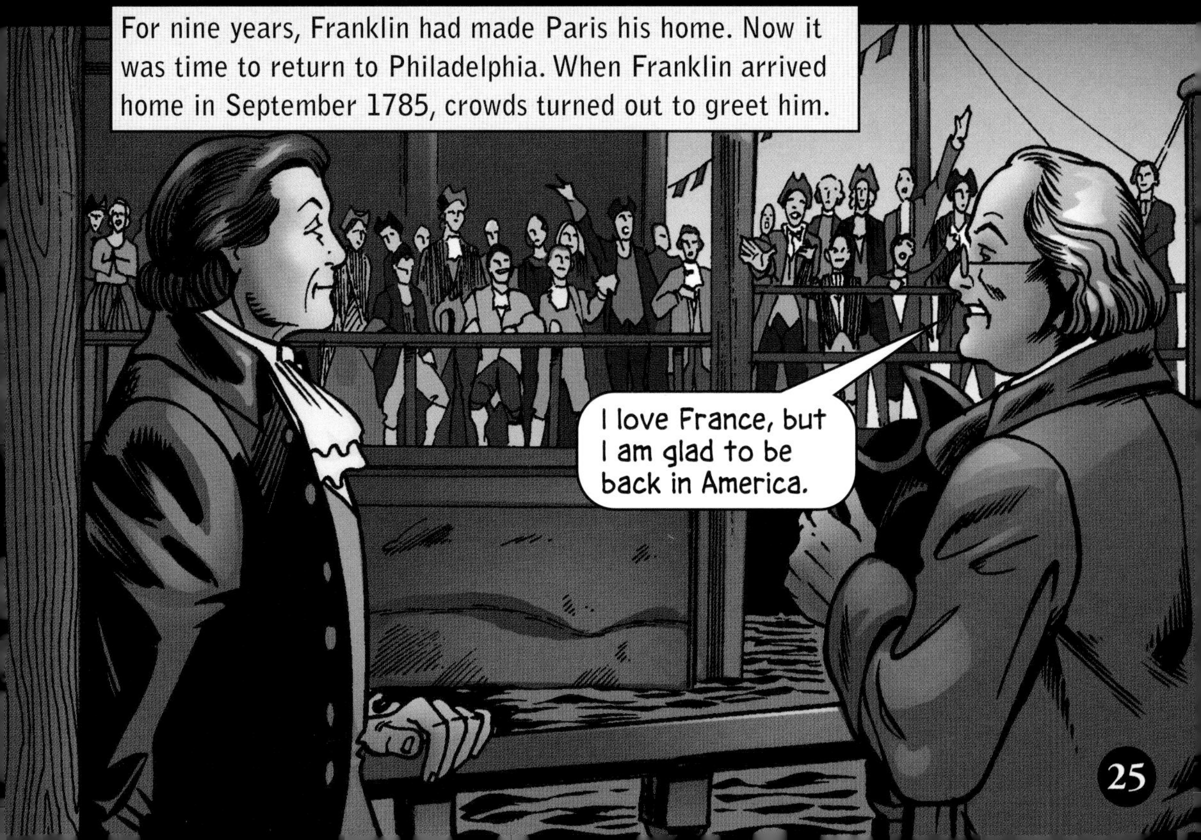
For nine years, Franklin had made Paris his home. Now it was time to return to Philadelphia. When Franklin arrived home in September 1785, crowds turned out to greet him.
I love France, but I am glad to be back in America.

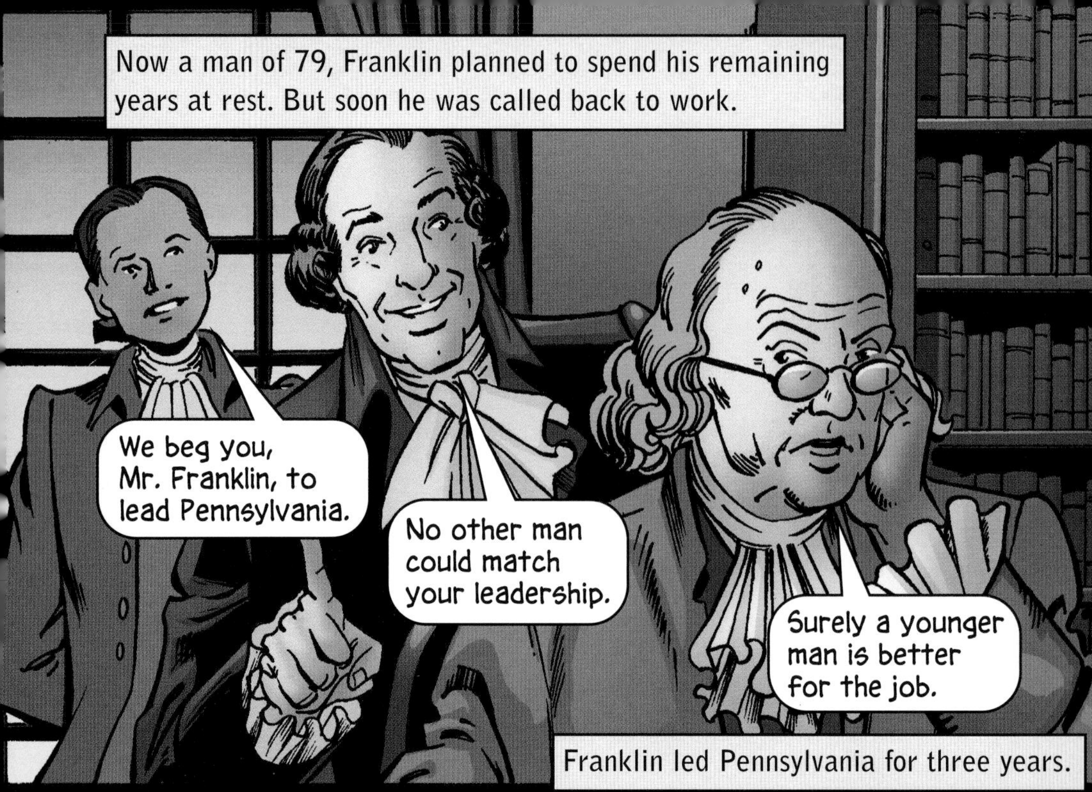
Now a man of 79, Franklin planned to spend his remaining years at rest. But soon he was called back to work.
We beg you, Mr. Franklin, to lead Pennsylvania.
No other man could match your leadership.
Surely a younger man is better for the job.
Franklin led Pennsylvania for three years.

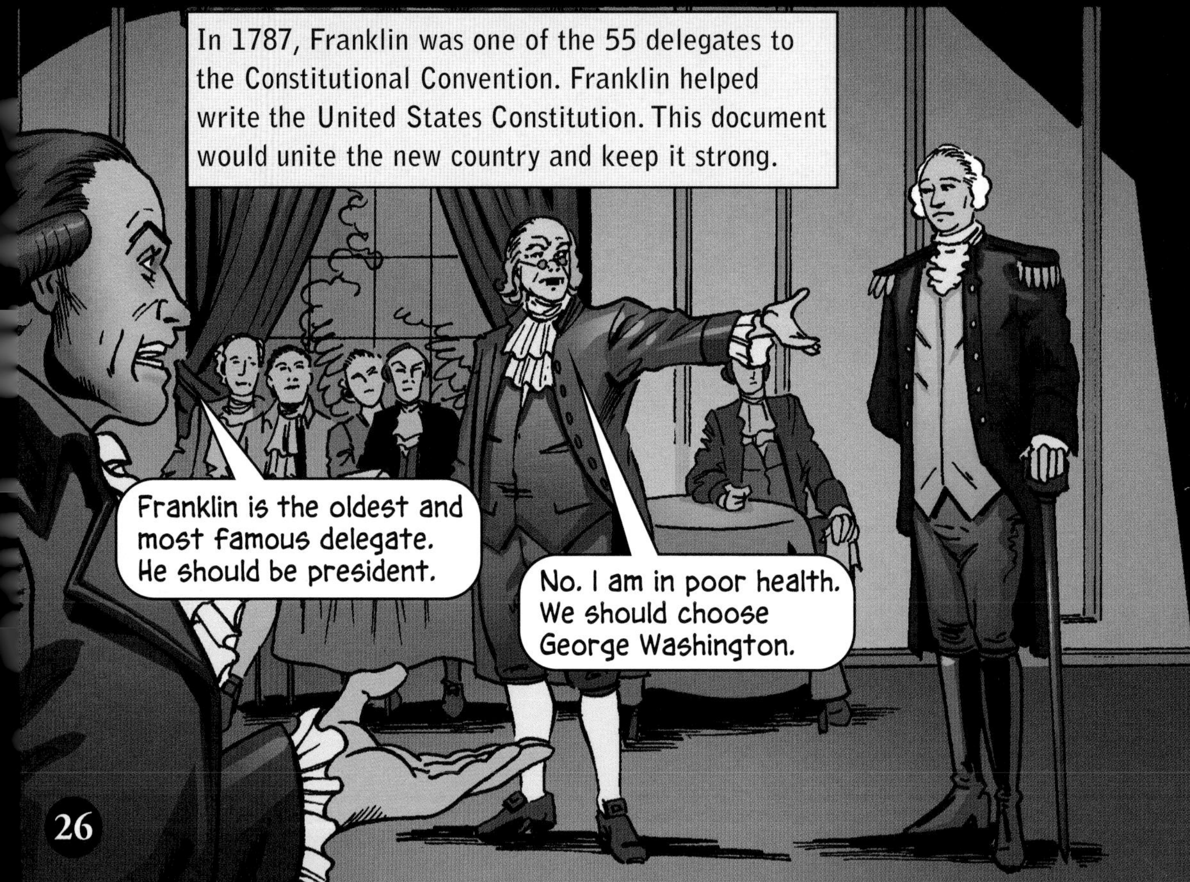
In 1787, Franklin was one of the 55 delegates to the Constitutional Convention. Franklin helped write the United States Constitution. This document would unite the new country and keep it strong.
Franklin is the oldest and most famous delegate. He should be president.
No. I am in poor health. We should choose George Washington.

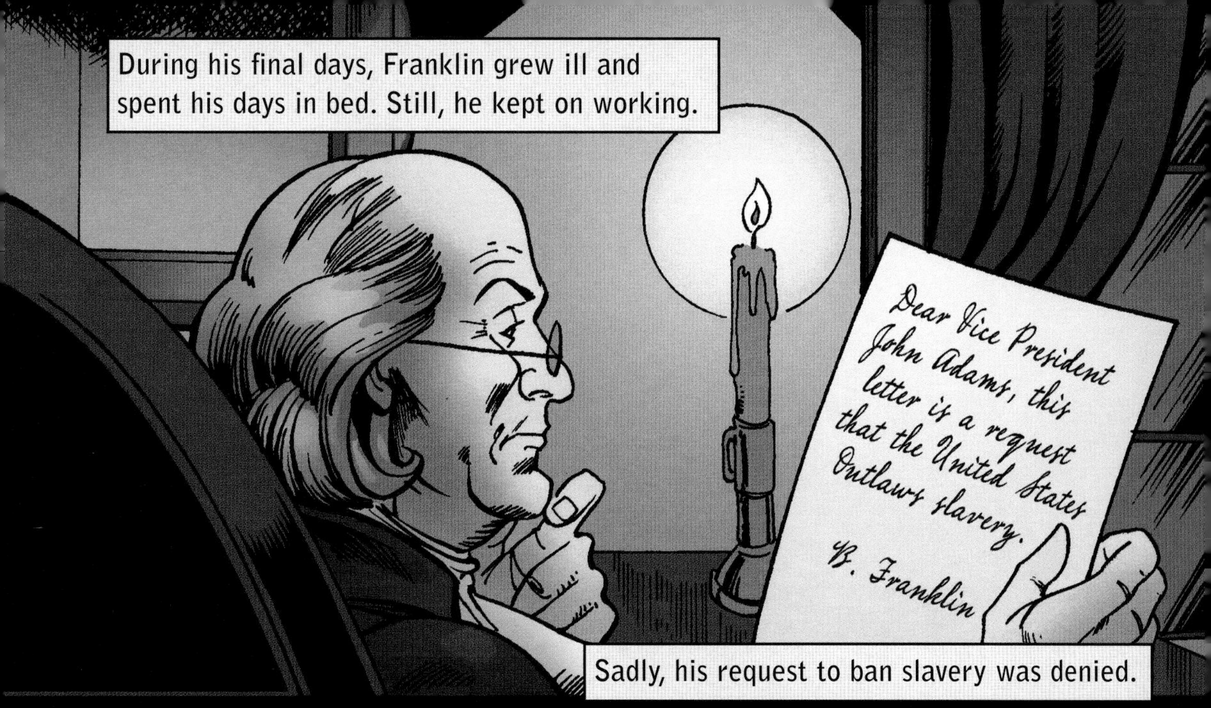

During his final days, Franklin grew ill and spent his days in bed. Still, he kept on working.
Dear Vice President John Adams, this letter is a request that the United States Outlaws slavery.
B. Franklin
Sadly, his request to ban slavery was denied.

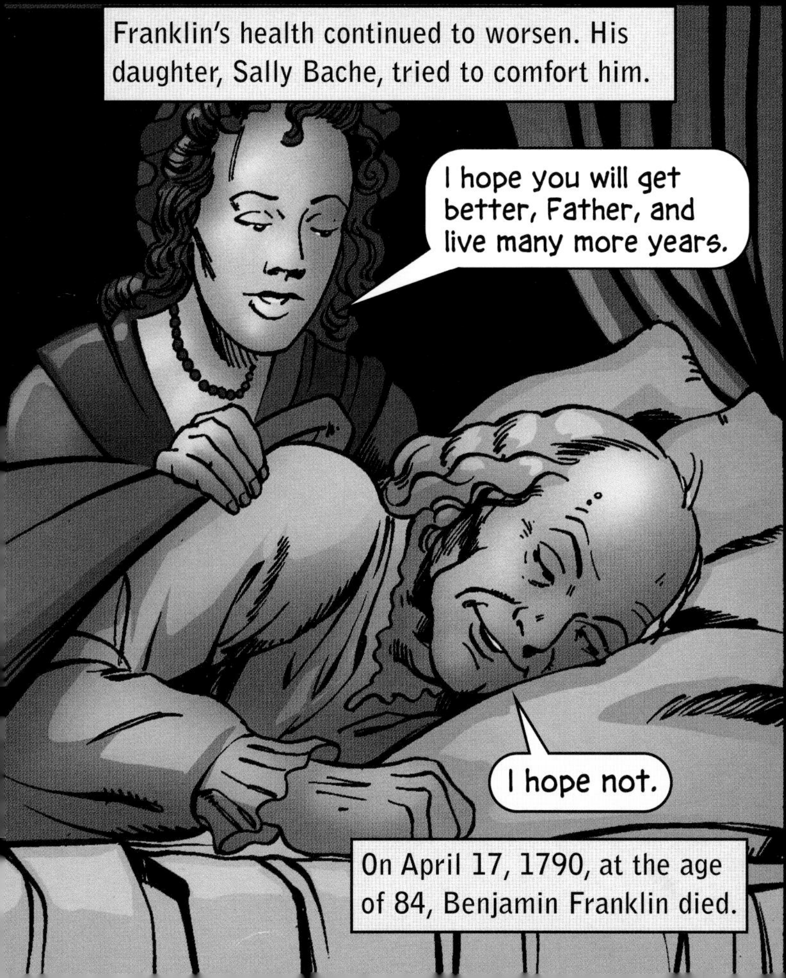

Franklin's health continued to worsen. His daughter, Sally Bache, tried to comfort him.
I hope you will get better, Father, and live many more years.
I hope not.
On April 17, 1790, at the age of 84, Benjamin Franklin died.

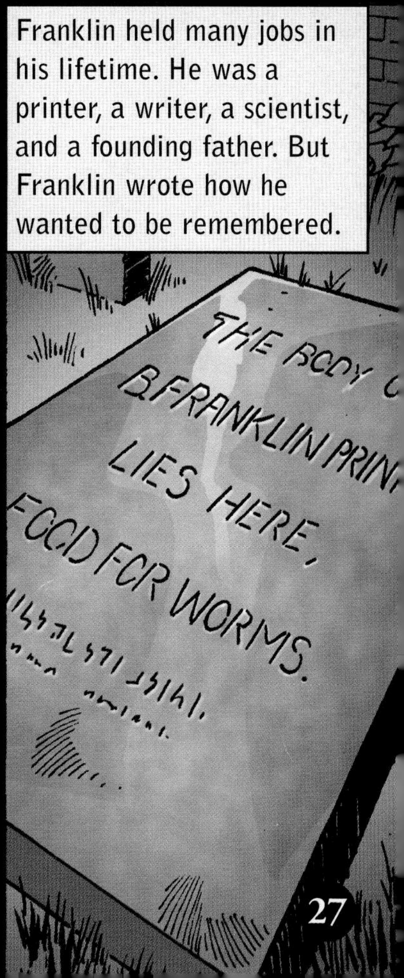

Franklin held many jobs in his lifetime. He was a printer, a writer, a scientist, and a founding father. But Franklin wrote how he wanted to be remembered.
THE BODY
B.FRANKLIN PRIN
LIES HERE,
FOOD FOR WORMS.

More about BENJAMIN FRANKLIN

- When Benjamin Franklin was 7 years old, he learned an important lesson about money. He bought a tin whistle. He soon tired of the whistle and thought of other things he could have bought. Later, Franklin said people's troubles most often came from "giving too much for the whistle."

- Franklin's first experiment with a kite had nothing to do with electricity. When he was 9 years old, Franklin floated on his back in a pond. He held on to a stick attached to a kite string. The wind carried the kite and pulled Franklin along in the water.

- Franklin had three children. His oldest son, William, became royal governor of New Jersey. Franklin's second son, Francis, died at age 4. His daughter, Sally, had seven children, including a son named Benjamin Franklin Bache.

- Franklin's *Poor Richard's Almanac* was published once a year from 1732 to 1758. Next to the Bible, it was the most read book in the colonies.

- During the Revolutionary War, Franklin's son William sided with the British, causing a disagreement with his father. William and Benjamin never made up.

- In 1771, Franklin began writing the story of his life. The pages were lost in 1777 when British soldiers used Franklin's house for their headquarters. One of Franklin's friends saw crumpled papers in the street and returned the pages to Franklin.

- In 1728, a young Franklin wrote how he wanted to be remembered. "The body of B. Franklin, Printer: (Like the cover of an old Book, Its contents torn out, and stripped of its Lettering & Gilding) Lies here, Food for Worms. But the Work shall not be lost: For it will, (as he believed) appear once more, In a new and more elegant Edition, Revised and corrected By the Author."

- Franklin is buried in Philadelphia. People often throw pennies on Franklin's grave for good luck.

- Franklin once wrote, "If you would not be forgotten as soon as you are dead and rotten, either write things worth reading, or do things worth the writing." Benjamin Franklin was a man who did both.

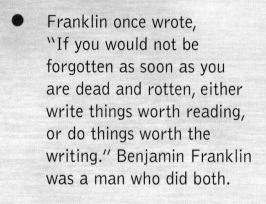

GLOSSARY

almanac (AWL-muh-nak)—a book published once a year with facts and statistics about a variety of subjects

apprentice (uh-PREN-tiss)—someone who learns a trade or craft by working with a skilled person

colony (KOL-uh-nee)—an area of land settled and governed by another country

delegate (DEL-uh-guht)—someone who represents other people at a meeting

dispute (diss-PYOOT)—a disagreement

treaty (TREE-tee)—an official agreement between two or more groups or countries

INTERNET SITES

FactHound offers a safe, fun way to find Internet sites related to this book. All of the sites on FactHound have been researched by our staff.

Here's how:

1. *Visit www.facthound.com*
2. Type in this special code **0736846298** for age-appropriate sites. Or enter a search word related to this book for a more general search.
3. Click on the **Fetch It** button.

FactHound will fetch the best sites for you!

READ MORE

Farshtey, Gregory T. *The American Revolution.* Daily Life. San Diego: Kidhaven Press, 2003.

Fleming, Candace. *Ben Franklin's Almanac: Being a True Account of the Good Gentleman's Life.* New York: Atheneum Books for Young Readers, 2003.

Graves, Kerry A. *The Declaration of Independence: The Story Behind America's Founding Document.* America in Words and Song. Philadelphia: Chelsea Clubhouse, 2004.

Riley, Gail Blasser. *Benjamin Franklin and Electricity.* Cornerstones of Freedom. New York: Children's Press, 2004.

BIBLIOGRAPHY

Franklin, Benjamin. *Poor Richard's Almanac.* Mount Vernon, N.Y.: Peter Pauper Press, 1980.

Franklin, Benjamin. *The Works of Benjamin Franklin,* edited by Jared Sparks. Boston: Hillard, Gray, and Company, 1840.

Franklin, Benjamin. *Writings,* edited by J. A. Leo Lemay. New York: Literary Classics of the United States: Distributed to the trade in the United States and Canada by Viking, 1987.

Van Doren, Carl. *Benjamin Franklin.* New York: Bramhall House, 1987.

INDEX